THE FIFTH ACT

INGMAR BERGMAN

Translated by
Linda Haverty Rugg and Joan Tate

The New Press
New York

© 1994 Cinematograph AB, Fårö.
Preface © 2001 by Lasse Bergström.
Monologue, After the Rehearsal, and
The Last Scream translation © 2001 by The New Press.
In the Presence of a Clown translation © 1997 by The Estate of Joan Tate. *In the Presence of a Clown* was revised for performance by the translator.
All rights reserved.
No part of this book may be reproduced, in any form,
without written permission from the publisher.

Published in the United States by The New Press, New York, 2001
Distributed by W.W. Norton & Company, Inc., New York

Library of Congress cataloging-in-publication data is available upon request.

The New Press was established in 1990 as a not-for-profit alternative to the large, commercial publishing houses currently dominating the book publishing industry. The New Press operates in the public interest rather than for private gain, and is committed to publishing, in innovative ways, works of educational, cultural, and community value that are often deemed insufficiently profitable.

The New Press, 450 West 41st Street, 6th floor, New York, NY 10036

www.thenewpress.com

Printed in the United States of America

2 4 6 8 10 9 7 5 3 1

CONTENTS

FOREWORD

At the beginning of 1994, when Ingmar Bergman assembled the texts that make up *The Fifth Act*, the recently composed piece *In the Presence of a Clown* existed only as a literary text. As Bergman writes in *Monologue*, his own introduction to the book, the play was conceived as a drama intended for the theater—the Royal Dramatic Theater in Stockholm—where Bergman is still very active.

But circumstances would have it otherwise. *In the Presence of a Clown* was produced a few years later as a television film, directed by an aged but vital Bergman who had declared back at the beginning of the 1980s that with *Fanny and Alexander* he had made his last film.

This was a natural development. Bergman has always been capable of contradicting his words through his actions. In *After the Rehearsal*, which he filmed for television with Lena Olin, Erland Josephsson, and Ingrid Thulin in 1983—the year after his grand farewell—he looks back at his life in the theater as if it had come to an end. And in *The Last Scream*, a one-act play about the forgotten Swedish filmmaker Georg af Klercker, a contemporary of Mauritz Stiller and Victor Sjöström, he portrays the artist's ultimate humiliation—to be robbed of the means of expression—in an apparently comic meeting between the artist and the economic powers-that-be. *The Last Scream* was written, produced on stage, and filmed. Naturally.

This black comedy, like *In the Presence of a Clown,* is about films, how films are made or cannot be made, and how films are experienced, until they literally burn up before the eyes of the audience.

A filmmaker and poet can never quit his art.

And Ingmar Bergman cannot, as he says in *Monologue,* quit writing. In his private studio he puts his ideas to paper, alone with his old-fashioned pen.

During his long career he has had an ambivalent relationship with his own role as author. He called his early film scripts "scores." For decades he hesitated to write the book that became *The Magic Lantern,* his memoirs, because it would have to be a finished product, not a snippet of prose between dramatic or cinematic scenes.

In the last decade of the last century he wrote three works about his parents, *Best Intentions, Sunday's Child,* and *Private Confessions.* They were filmed by others—*Best Intentions* by Bille August, *Sunday's Child* by his son Daniel Bergman, and *Private Confessions* by Liv Ullmann, one of the women in his life.

It is conceivable that these films will sink into oblivion and finally be remembered only as literary works. In that case Ingmar Bergman would be astonished, but not his readers or his publishers.

Lasse Bergström
Stockholm
October 2000

PEER GYNT.   Away with you, fear! Get a grip, old man!

I don't want to die! I must get to land!

THE PASSENGER.   Don't worry your grizzled head about that—

You won't die in the middle of the final act.
(*Glides away*)

MONOLOGUE

The lights come up.

Close-up of an older gray-bearded man. During a long silence he regards his invisible audience. He begins to speak in fits and starts. He is no speaker.

To read silently has been difficult for me for as long as I can remember. I read carefully, slowly. If I try to pick up the pace, the whole thing falls apart at once: I lose the thread. Irrelevant fragments of thoughts and feelings flicker across the pages, and I am forced to start over. I think, in fact, that I read silently at just about the same pace that I read aloud. A three-hundred-page novel has a running time of about six weeks, assuming that I immerse myself for an hour each day. A normal play—whatever that means—takes one to two weeks. Shakespeare takes longer.

But that's not the worst of it.

Certain texts never come clear, even if I read them in my mother tongue. I tried, for instance, to drag myself through Ernst Deutsch's Trotsky biography and got depressed and frustrated because I simply did not grasp the text's meaning. Peter Weiss was a friend of mine. I put on a production of his oratorio *The Investigation*. But his novel, *The Aesthetics of Resistance*, remained impenetrable even after repeated attempts. Botho Strauss is incomprehensible in spots, both in German and in excellent translations. But his theater pieces are never difficult. I move freely and contentedly through the combinations of letters, sentences, lines, and scenes, which, like music, speak to my intuition.

When I am forced sometimes to read aloud from a book, it comes out in a stumbling monotone, rife with errors. It has always been that way, despite the fact that my grandmother taught me the art of reading when I was five.

Unlike the ability, the desire to read has always been with me. A library, a bookstore, a new book, an old, old book, an unknown or for that matter a well-known play radiates a magnetic force, sometimes magic. But then I say to myself: "Wittgenstein" or "Lacan." After two pages of confusion and rage, I think: Am I suffering from some essential flaw in my ability to comprehend, or what?

Slow reading has one advantage, a professional one. When I work through a dramatic text, I see and hear the transubstantiated words very clearly. Usually I decide on a staging during that first confrontation. I *know* that this is *my* text, even though it contains granite blocks of unsolvable problems.

It never occurred to me that I would write in either poetry or prose. The summer of 1940 brought an end to that notion. For a long time I had been living under repulsive circumstances. That September I was offered a chance to wrest myself from the jaws of depression and reality, while living in a little garret in my grandparents' summer house in the western province of Dalarna. After tramping endlessly through my childhood landscape, its light and smells, I began to put words to paper. It was a sensation never before experienced. A desire that detonated so silently and mildly. In less than two months I wrote twelve plays. One of these attempts at theater was produced at the Student Theater. It was an unabashed, to say the least, plagiarism of Strindberg's *Kasper's Fat Tuesday*. The production at the student union was a success. This led in its turn to full-time employment as a "script peon" at the Swedish Film Industry. There were six of us slaves, each of whom had command over a hole in the wall in the attic of the establishment, equipped with a desk and a telephone. Our boss and mentor was Stina

Bergman, the widow of novelist Hjalmar Bergman. Our task—between nine and five—was to edit, finish, polish, and perhaps even write film scripts. The volume was colossal. The company produced twenty-five films a year. Only a fraction of a considerable number of finished scripts went into production. At the same time I continued to write plays for the theater. Some of them were printed and published. Some were produced.

For the most part the reviews were disheartening. I was told that I was a talented director but a deplorable writer. After re-reading what remains of my dramatic production, I am prepared to agree with my critics. My idols were Strindberg, whom I began to consume at the age of twelve, and Hjalmar Bergman, whom I discovered somewhat later. My perpetual insecurity resulted in an attempt to write like both Strindberg and Bergman. Page after page of Strindberg's bombastic dialogue, page after page of Bergman's intoxicating verbal virtuosity. The absence of any personal style shone through. Gradually publishers and theater directors tired of me, and I was unanimously rejected, which was irritating at the time. Today I am mostly grateful.

The consequence was logical. My way into short stories, novels, and drama was hermetically sealed. Only film remained. The advantages were clear. Swedish film scripts were without exception bad, if not miserable, wretchedly miserable. No one demanded any literary credentials. If ever a "real author" threw together a film script, it was a question of pressing economic need or a fondness for the lovely ladies of the profession. I found my place. Mostly by editing other people's books and stories, sometimes by writing my own, like *Torment* and *Prison*.

Our sole reigning model was American dramaturgy: clarity, order, plainness, structure. It was something you could build on. Gradually, as a sense of security began to take hold, you could do a takeoff on the form, turn it around.

And so I was allowed to continue to write, without anybody

giving a damn about *how* I wrote. It was the finished film that counted. The script was a half-finished product, like a musical score, at best. Bit by bit I dared to try and attempt expressions of my own. It was, fortunately, enough, almost unnoticeable and an enormous pleasure. On the face of things the script looked as I had been taught scripts should look: clear divisions into scenes and lines, specific instructions about set design, lights, wardrobe, and props. *Persona* was the first film in which I cut loose and dared simply to write a story. When people asked me when I intended to produce a script, I explained that *this* was the script and that no so-called shooting script was planned.

One of the pleasant results of fame was that foreign editors wanted to publish my writing. Even Swedes expressed an interest. My stockpiled bitterness rose to the surface, and I accepted the foreign offers and refused the Swedish ones. This attitude was a blend of my wounded pride and secret coquetry. The outcome: several of my films exist in foreign languages, while the originals have disappeared. I did not even hold on to the director's copy. So it goes.

The close-up switches to a medium shot. Now we can see that the man is leaning on a stool. His attitude is more embarrassed than anything else. Despite this, he continues his speech.

So I am a lousy reader, but I take pleasure in it. I write slowly and carefully, make changes, rewrite, make more changes. That gives me pleasure, too. I cannot draw—not even a stick figure. Scenographers regard with bemused tolerance my attempts to explain through drawing what I want in set design and other visual elements. My love for music is unrequited. I lack an ear or memory for melody. But it doesn't much matter. The most important thing is not to be loved, but to love. If I had been talented and had not become what I have become, I would have in all probability been a musical director. It's true that I'm completely deaf in my right ear since my military duty, when I was in charge of a so-called machine gun, model fourteen. But my left ear can still hear a cricket sing. My right eye is what they call legally blind, but I can see like a raven with the left one. In the performance of my profession, I am capable, untiring, and orderly.

I often think of Death, several times a day. It has become a habit, probably part of aging. Sometimes my fear grows into a panic, other times I think I have solved the riddle and feel an unfamiliar sense of well-being, as if I had entered into a fragile peace treaty with life.

A brief close-up that does not conform to the previous one, either in terms of lighting or camera perspective. The image was apparently taken on a later occasion. The old man seems disoriented.

I forgot to point out—maybe I should have pointed out that all of this talking is an attempt to describe—I don't know what I should call it, possibly a "handicap" if that doesn't sound too dramatic, since my disabilities, I mean my problems with reading, writing, drawing, and music are only painful at moments. Sometimes it has seemed to me that the difficulties I've described were what made me into a passable professional. Other factors have also played a role, and all of that can be found, by the way, in *After the Rehearsal*, which is an honest attempt to be honest. Now I can't think of anything more to say.

The close-up is broken by an extreme long shot, which shows the speaker's surroundings, a theater stage of course, cluttered with a half-changed set, most likely from that day's rehearsal of the evening performance. A bell pings monotonously; it is the signal warning of the slowly falling iron curtain, which stops half way (is it intentional, metaphorical, symbolic?). The lighting of this staged chaos is just as carefully effective: darkness up under the roof, the horizontal line of the proscenium softly delineated, the cyclorama gently illuminated, individual objects clearly defined. The protagonist is still standing in the same place, leaning against a stool.

I wrote the texts in this book without giving a thought to their possible media, using a method something like that of the harpsichord sonatas by Bach—though they are otherwise not comparable. They can be played by string quartets, wind ensembles, guitar, organ, or piano. I wrote them in the way I have been accustomed to writing for more than fifty years—it looks like drama but could just as easily be film, television, or simply texts for reading. It was by chance that *After the Rehearsal* was made into a film for television and that *The Last Scream* was produced for the stage. It was also my intention that *In the Presence of a Clown* should be played in the theater.

The wide-angled long shot shifts to a final close-up. Perhaps I forgot to mention that the film is in black and white. The old gentleman has probably been told to say a little more about his book. He seems relieved, since the monologue is apparently nearing its end.

The Fifth Act deals with my indefatigable companions: the stage, actors and film, movie theaters, cinematography. They have been by my side ever since I built my first puppet theater under the white table in our childhood playroom and, several years later, moved into a roomy closet along with a little tin machine equipped with a crank, a Maltese cross, a lens, a paraffin lamp, and a sepia roll of film.

Over the years the circumstances and the settings have become—how should I say it—grander, but the *feeling* itself is undeniably the same.

What do I mean by "feeling"?

Passion?

Pleasure?

Love?

Obsession? It sounds overblown, but maybe that's it: Obsession.

Fade to black. Credits. Music: "The Merry Widow Waltz."

—Fårö, July 18, 1994

AFTER
THE REHEARSAL

An old theater. Afternoon. A gray, indirect light sifts in through unseen shutters, leaving the ceiling and firewall in darkness. Uneven floor. Curtain half-raised. Stage partially cluttered with objects, props, and scrims left standing from the afternoon's rehearsal, which ended just an hour ago. The big house seems drained of people.

Near the ramp stands a worn, old armchair that's played a role in many Ibsen plays. In the armchair sits a motionless HENRIK VO-GLER; *he looks almost stuffed. He is 109 years old, or maybe just sixty-two. Next to him is a music stand holding an open copy of the play. Its pages are scribbled over with illegible notes, arrows, and crosses. Nothing happens for a long while. Then the sound of footsteps. A door opens and closes somewhere deep in the darkness of the stage:* ANNA EGERMAN *slowly enters the ramp's sleepy circle of light. She moves through the objects and furniture, looking for something on the illuminated set. At first she doesn't see* VOGLER.

VOGLER What are you looking for?

ANNA (*laughs*) You scared me, I didn't see you! (*Pause*) I'm looking for my watch. I'm the kind of person who loses things.

VOGLER Valuable?

ANNA Not to me, but to the person who gave it to me.

VOGLER I see.

ANNA So I wear it for him. He'll be so—

VOGLER—sad—mad—inconsolable—jealous—despairing—cold—suspicious—miserable?

ANNA (*laughs*) More or less. (*Pause*) Why are you sitting here, anyway?

VOGLER Because I enjoy it.

ANNA I heard you didn't like evening rehearsals.

VOGLER No. Evenings are for performances.

ANNA And yet you didn't give us this evening off.

VOGLER The canceled performance gives us an extra chance to be onstage. We have to take advantage of that. You had other plans for this evening, I suppose.

ANNA Peter and I were going to—(*stops herself*)

VOGLER (*smiles*) That's really none of my business.

ANNA (*after a pause*) It was nothing special.

VOGLER Oh, no?

ANNA I'd be happy to rehearse all day.

VOGLER There's no need for apologies.

ANNA I'm not apologizing, I'm just trying—

VOGLER How old are you anyway, Anna Egerman?

ANNA Guess!

VOGLER You're the same age as my youngest daughter. Your father and I were making a film together, and each of us was blessed with a daughter, a week apart. The happy events were greeted with a thorough celebration. You are twenty-three years and three months old, right?

ANNA You and Papa used to have fun back then.

VOGLER Do I hear a hint of accusation in your voice? Both of us had a big family to support. Besides, we thought our work was fun. It was as natural as breathing.

ANNA Papa was always gone and Mama was always sad. She was an unusually good actress. Wasn't she?

VOGLER Your mother was one of the most beautiful women I've ever seen: enchanting, highly talented, and passionate. Then she married Michael and left the theater.

ANNA You were in love with Mama, too.

VOGLER Naturally.

ANNA Did you have an affair?

VOGLER No. (*Short laugh*)

ANNA Why not?

VOGLER There was a strong inner tension between us. We must have thought that the tension was good for our work. Why does an infatuation become an affair? Usually because of thoughtlessness, optimism, politeness, or misunderstanding. Your mother and I kept our distance from each other. Your father was more courageous or more foolhardy, but that's how things turned out the way they did.

ANNA Mama produced a pack of children that she didn't like. She made two serious attempts at suicide and died of alcohol poisoning. Once I asked her why she had left the theater. She answered that she loved Papa and didn't want to squander her life. It sounded beautiful, anyway. Mama was such an unbeliev-able liar.

VOGLER It's strange to hear you speak of your mother.

ANNA (*smiles*) Do you think I'm too harsh?

VOGLER I think you don't understand her.

ANNA How am I supposed to pretend to be understanding when I don't understand. It took me many years to dare to hate her completely. Until I could, I walked around with a terrible anguish that nearly made me feebleminded. Now I hate her and feel much better. And where she is now, she can hardly be concerned about that anymore.

VOGLER (*smiles*) That's the great question, of course.

ANNA I read in an interview somewhere where you were explaining that this is our only life, that a "before" and especially an "afterward" did not exist. You said that science had offered you the greatest comfort.

VOGLER You are certainly a girl with a gift for irony.

ANNA I'm just confused.

VOGLER When a person is going full speed, the final darkness seems distant. Then suddenly you start to count your performances backwards.

ANNA You don't mean that.

VOGLER My father was a parson. When he was old and sick, I asked him how he felt about dying. He said: I am a little frightened.

ANNA (*suddenly laughs*) Here I sit, talking with an old friend of Papa's about death.

VOGLER Weren't you terribly thin and short, with long black hair, like a troll? Your brothers and sisters were friendly and approachable, but you were rather sullen.

ANNA You were at our house often, weren't you? Why did you disappear so suddenly? Did you become enemies?

VOGLER Not enemies, precisely.

ANNA You're not going to tell me what it was all about, I can hear it in your voice.

VOGLER I'm going to tell you something, Anna Egerman. Just lean forward, and suddenly you'll find your head plunged into another dimension! The dead are not dead, the living behave like ghosts. What was obvious a minute ago is strange and impenetrable. Anna! Listen to the silence here on the stage. Think of the spiritual energy, all the feelings, genuine and acted, laughter and rage and passions and who knows what. All of that is still here, enclosed in this space, living its secret, uninterrupted life. Sometimes I hear them, often I hear them, sometimes I think I see them. Demons, angels, ghosts, ordinary people, they are completely preoccupied with their own affairs, they turn away from us, in their own secret world. Sometimes we speak to one another but only in passing, by chance. Now you're smiling that wonderfully ironic smile.

ANNA My smile is not at all ironic. I think that what you're saying sounds beautiful. I understand what you mean with the silence of the stage. But do you really believe that—

VOGLER Does it matter? If it is like a dream, in which I create entire performances with actors and lines, or if they really live their own lives outside and beyond my senses? Isn't it all the same?

ANNA And yet you believe that my mother suffers from my hate, despite the fact that she has been dead for five years.

VOGLER You frighten me when you speak of your hate. I believe that your hate reaches her, strikes her.

ANNA If I have to be honest, if you're right about that, I'm glad.

Vogler wants to say something but stops himself.

ANNA You were going to say something.

VOGLER You are acting a role and it is your play.

Silence.

ANNA Why did you want me to play Indra's Daughter?

VOGLER Because you're talented.

ANNA (*laughs*) Really?

VOGLER I saw you playing Agnes in a student production of *Brand*. You were terrible.

ANNA I was terrible.

VOGLER Only someone with talent can act that badly. And then I saw you in a film. It was not an especially remarkable role and the film was bad. I had just received the offer to come here and produce something. When I saw you in that film I thought: I can put on *The Dream Play* with Anna Egerman as Agnes. It felt fun and right and it will be my fifth *Dream Play*. Maybe there will be a sixth and a seventh. When I was twelve years old I got to go along with a musician who played the organ backstage. It was an explosive experience. Night after night, hidden up among the stage lights, I witnessed the marriage scene between the Lawyer and the Daughter. It was the first time I experienced the actor's magic. The Lawyer held a hairpin between his thumb and forefinger. He twisted it, straightened it out, and broke it in two. There was no hairpin, but I saw it! The Officer stood backstage, waiting for his entrance. He was leaning down, looking at his shoes, his hands on his back, soundlessly clearing his throat, an entirely ordinary person. Suddenly he opens the door and enters the light onstage. He is transformed, he is the Officer. It was up there that it all began. (*He points to the lights.*) There I sat, huddled behind two spotlights and the piece of metal they used to make thunder.

ANNA I'm too young for the part.

VOGLER Anyone who plays Indra's Daughter is either too young or too old. The role is essentially unplayable.

ANNA You always used to cut the script and edit it—

VOGLER It's easiest that way: I don't understand *this*—let's throw out this crap. *This* is just ridiculous, I'll rewrite it. *This* scene is not where it should be; I'll move it. I knead the text with a specific purpose in mind. In the finale I'll raise a gigantic cross, or put a hundred extras out there to fill the stage, wearing shabby clothes and raising their left fists in the air. I rape Strindberg. It is very easy and very fashionable. The critics praise me: I've blown the dust off the old fogy. It's only theater people who can allow themselves this kind of sloppy rape. It would be unthinkable in a musical performance, partly because it's impossible to misinterpret notation, partly because the musical profession demands expertise. Any idiot can mess with Ibsen, but no one would dare defile Mozart, because he would catch hell from the critics and the audience. I have now decided to play *The Dream Play* as written. I will reproduce every word, every moment, every scene as I imagine Strindberg saw it. It is an exercise in futility, since many of the scenes are impossible to realize. For instance, our titan Strindberg had bad taste. He arranged a few dusty palm trees in one corner of his dining room, and in the palms he hung colored lights. In the evenings his sister came and played Beethoven's sonatas. They turned on the lights and sat down in his palm grove with his punch and his cigar. His *Dream Play* is marred by several illuminations of that ilk.

Oh, I'm rambling. You want me to convince you that you're right for the role, that's my task, that's the delicious secret of our relationship: you require that I believe in you and you demand constant reassurance. If I am sufficiently convincing on the verbal, emotional, and intellectual planes, in the end you will finally believe me and allow your self-confidence to bloom. I in my turn am stimulated by your faith in me. I am struck with inspiration, which in turn can be good for you. You show your spontaneous gratitude. I am seized by a slight dizziness and think: Thank you, Lord, for allowing the miracle to descend on us once more. Blood pulses, tiny little blood vessels filled with reddest life branch out to the farthest, saddest edge of the company, coloring the cheeks of the mediocre and lighting their eyes.

That's how it is, Anna Egerman. That's how it has to be. When I first saw you, a little black-haired troll on your Papa's knee, I might have thought, that one will be an actress, she refuses to accept reality; when I saw you as that terrible Agnes in *Brand* I thought, only a really talented actress would be this bad; when I saw you in that stupid film, when I saw the way you carried yourself, the way you spoke, when I saw your eyes, your impatience and your vulnerability, it made me happy and I felt that with you, I would be able once again to move the rock that has gotten heavier and heavier with the years. (*Falls silent and sits there, gray.*)

ANNA (*after a pause*) If it is as you say, I don't understand why you're so critical of me. You change everything I do. Sometimes I cry with despair when I get home. I don't believe that you believe in me at all.

VOGLER An actor who doesn't believe in his director has many ways to show it. He doesn't listen, he humiliates the director by following his instructions to the point of exaggeration, he protests every suggestion and launches endless arguments, he gets aggressive and insults the director in front of his colleagues. A director who doesn't believe in his actor can be very encouraging. He can also remain passive, which drives the actor into a nervous breakdown. He makes use of his advantage, which is that the actor has to expose himself under the lights while the director remains in the darkness of the auditorium. He makes a fool of the actor, exhorts him to think, not to think, to control himself, to let go, to be natural, to be stylized, and so on. A director can kill an actor—and that is not so unusual—but an actor can also kill a director. You don't believe that I believe in you, Anna Egerman. That is the only stupid thing I've heard you say in the five weeks we've been rehearsing. You say that you cry, but if I may hazard a guess, I think you cry with pleasure. You know that something is happening inside you: a redistribution and a restructuring of your resources. It's happening in a practical and tangible way, which may be a little painful, but at the same time makes you happy and satisfied. When we talk to each other outside rehearsal, you're a much worse actress than when we're working. Get rid of the private actress! She is just stealing a lot of strength from the real actress and standing in the way of impulses that you could use on the stage. (*Falls silent and sits there, gray.*)

ANNA Well, *that* was a lecture.

VOGLER Yes.

ANNA So you think that I'm acting in my private life.

Vogler doesn't answer, shrugs.

ANNA People are grateful when you show them the face they expect to see. A person who gives you a gift or shows you a kindness wants you to show them happiness. When someone wants you to show love or tenderness, you get love in return. You're supposed to show sympathy, be funny or sexy or sad. Are you always genuine?

VOGLER Me! (*He runs a hand over his face.*) I live a rather isolated life.

ANNA And at our rehearsals?

VOGLER It's not about my feelings, but yours and the other actors' feelings. I use any and every means to get you to function. That is my profession. And my only real happiness, besides. (*He looks at her.*)

ANNA Is it important to be careful with feelings? And with the expression of feelings? If I didn't have my private little drama, how could I protect myself from the outside world?

VOGLER Guess.

ANNA Maybe I shouldn't protect myself?

Vogler looks at her, smiles weakly.

ANNA Who was it that tricked me into using feigned feelings? It must have begun early. A long way back in childhood. Playing the coquette, the need to be please everyone. Mama could be pretty frightening, and Papa—

VOGLER You know all of that.

ANNA As a child you are the underling, and you just keep it up out of inertia. Because it's easier. (*Suddenly*) I have to ask you about something important.

Vogler nods.

ANNA In the marriage scene with the Lawyer, you have me walk back and forth like an animal in a cage. Apparently I can't do it the way you want at all. I feel pretty silly.

VOGLER Try it a little bit longer. If it doesn't work, we'll think of something else.

ANNA Maria got a lot of praise for that pacing in your earlier production, eleven years ago. But I'm not nearly as good as she is, and besides, she was twice as old as I am and—

VOGLER Have you read those reviews?

ANNA Of course.

Vogler laughs.

ANNA What's so funny about that? Maria is dead and she's a legend. I have to know something about who I'm—

VOGLER If you don't want to pace around like Maria, why don't you do the opposite? Sit motionlessly, as if chained to the chair, right next to the stove, since she's supposed to be freezing. Don't get up until the Officer comes to free you from your prison, and then you can get up as if you had been paralyzed. It will be very effective. And Maria will roll over in her grave.

ANNA So I'll sit motionlessly, but I can reach out to him when I say "Beloved! I am dying in this air, in this room, with the view onto a backyard, with babies shrieking for endless sleepless hours, with these people out there and their misery, strife, and accusations. I will have to die in here." And then he comes up to me and embraces me and falls on his knees by the chair and says "Poor little flower." Yes, that will probably work. It would be a colossal help. A few days ago you said that the Daughter is heavy, hundreds of pounds in that scene. But I can't find any weight.

VOGLER The weight should be in your hips and shoulders.

ANNA Yes, that's what you say, but—

VOGLER It's not so easy when you're bouncing with lust for life. You even have trouble standing still during the Departure scene. Stand still, enjoy standing, and stand with your whole body, not just with your legs.

ANNA (*looks at him*) How would you know that? You've never been an actor.

VOGLER I once asked a Catholic priest how he could know anything about relations between a man and a woman. He answered that you don't have to be a murderer to be able to sense something of the murderer's psychology.

ANNA But you might have to be a butcher to know how to cut up a pig.

VOGLER I have a little butcher in me.

ANNA How can you be so sure that you use the right words with an actor?

VOGLER I can feel it.

ANNA Aren't you ever afraid that your feelings are wrong?

VOGLER When I was younger and should have had reason to be afraid, I didn't grasp that I had reason to be afraid.

ANNA Many directors make their careers on a road paved with slaughtered actors. Have you ever cared enough to count your victims?

VOGLER No.

ANNA Maybe you don't have any victims.

VOGLER I don't think so.

ANNA How can you be so sure?

VOGLER In life, or shall we say reality, I believe that there are many people who bear the scars of my reckless drive, just as I bear the marks of the actions of others.

ANNA But not in the theater?

VOGLER No. Not in the theater. You wonder how I can be so sure, so now I will tell you something that sounds both sentimental and exaggerated, but is the pure truth, anyway: I love the actors. I love them as a phenomenon, I love their profession, I love their courage or contempt for death or whatever you want to call it. I understand their need for escape but also their ruthless honesty. I love it when they try to manipulate me and I envy them their gullibility and their insight. I love the actors, and so I can never hurt them. My old teacher once said to me: A director must learn two things, he has to learn to listen and to keep his mouth shut. Actors are creative artists, but not particularly verbal. You have to listen, be patient and wait. You can't talk the actor's often uncertain and unclear ideas into the ground.

ANNA You say quite a bit to me.

VOGLER You're a beginner, that's another story. I have to weed your garden a little. There are quite a few weeds in there. But the roses are incomparable. (*Yawns*)

ANNA Are you tired?

VOGLER I usually take a little nap at this time in the afternoon. My blood sugar is at its lowest now.

ANNA Were you going to sit here and fall asleep?

VOGLER No, I was going to sit here and get sentimental.

ANNA Then I don't want to disturb you.

VOGLER If I remember correctly, you weren't wearing a watch this morning. Now I remember that I noticed particularly that you were not wearing your watch.

ANNA (*laughs*) Is that so?

VOGLER Anyway, you don't disturb me in the least, and there's no way you can stop my desire to be sentimental. On the contrary.

ANNA Then I'll sit down here.

VOGLER Come a little closer so that I can see you better, my dear, said the wolf to Red Riding Hood. That hairstyle suits you, by the way.

ANNA I've let my hair grow out for the part.

VOGLER For the first few days you had some modern—I don't know what, but it wasn't right for you, anyway.

ANNA I thought I should look a little stylish for your sake, so I went to the hairdresser. It was a big mistake.

VOGLER For my sake? Why, thank you.

ANNA It was all about making an impression, you understand.

VOGLER I didn't think that a young, self-sufficient, modern—

ANNA (*happily*) In that way I'm not particularly modern.

VOGLER So you're going to sit there on the sofa. Then I'll come over to you. (*Gets up*) Hell! I have such a damned pain in my leg.

ANNA Have you had it for a long time?

VOGLER It's death, you understand. It's nibbling at me like an eager little rat.

ANNA Are you and Papa the same age?

VOGLER Yes, that's the way it is. We are the same age. And now we're sitting here.

ANNA And looking out over the dark auditorium—

VOGLER—surrounded by darkened spotlights, the dust is falling over our heads from the darkness of the eaves. Under us—

ANNA—under us an abyss of machines for the revolving stage and the sinking stage and trap doors and—

VOGLER And so we sit here on this sofa, perfectly proper, this sofa that looks so inviting but has been especially made so that you can't sink too far into it—the armchair over there played a role in *Hedda Gabler* and the sofa appeared in *The Father*. I used that table in *Tartuffe*, the chairs in my last *Dream Play*.

Just a few acquaintances of mine. I greet them like old friends.
It makes me feel safe that they are here, that they allow themselves to be used from performance to performance. I like my
rehearsal screens best. They remind me of my childhood. I had
a big wooden box with the most basic kind of blocks. They
could be anything I wanted. For me, this is best: table, chair,
screen, stage, work lights, actors in everyday clothes, voices,
movement, faces, stillness. Magic. Everything *represents*, nothing *is*. The understanding between actor and audience. The
best theater that ever was was Shakespeare's theater. They
played in daylight, and when they wanted to make it night they
brought torches onto the stage and the oboes played a leitmo-
tif. Night: oboes, torches. This rubbish that we bring onstage!
Every time I say that I'm going to— Boring, Anna! Boring! I
love these old theaters, they're like violins, incredibly sensi-
tive, refined, definitive. But they restrain us. A theater performance occurs if three elements are at hand: the words, the
actor, the audience. That's all you need, those are the only
things needed for the miracle to take effect.

This is my conviction, my deepest conviction, but I have
never followed it. I am much too bound to this depraved,
dusty, shitty instrument. (*Gestures toward the stage*) That's how
it is and how it's always been.

ANNA Is it a question of morality?

VOGLER I think that our art is moral. By moral I mean bound by
law. If you break the law you will be punished and the punish-
ment is unambiguous: you will not reach your audience. The
receiver will remain mute, indifferent, passive. You will act in
vain, you have no justification for your existence, you could
just as well be dead.

ANNA So an actor who fails to reach his audience is an immoral
person.

VOGLER A true actor will always reach them. He reaches them
despite his role, the other actors, the director, and the set: he

touches them, worries them, lives. My old teacher divided actors into two categories: one goes in, the other goes out.

ANNA That sounds unfair.

VOGLER It's not fair, but it isn't equal, either. You don't give a hang about Andersson no matter what he does, while you watch Pettersson even if he is standing farthest away on the stage and does not say a word.

ANNA Not everyone can be a genius.

VOGLER No, but everybody can be trained. They have to know how they can produce effect in the best way, they have to govern their technique, both spiritual and physical. For example, they have to learn that they have ears. Ears to listen with. The best conductors get the best musicians to listen *to each other*. The fine first-class actor broadens his sense of self to embrace not only the person he is acting with at that moment but all of his fellow actors. He has to establish a sensual relationship in the deepest meaning of that term. Long ago, in the bad old days, the theater schools were associated with the big theaters. Initiates were pulled right into the general circulation system. From the beginning they got to listen to their older colleagues, to admire, despise, imitate. They got their first silent roles, then their first lines. They lived the life of the theater. The older people were their teachers not only in the classroom but, most importantly, on the stage. Today some murdering bureaucrat has cut off our circulation. The students are raised like broiler chickens in more or less hermetically sealed-off schools. It's not much of a surprise that the results are bad. You were lucky, Anna Egerman. Both of your parents were actors. You have lived with the theater since you began breathing. You are a Princess of the Blood.

ANNA I didn't want to become an actress.

VOGLER Who forced you?

ANNA I thought: I'm not going to be like Mama. Sometimes when they were fighting I stood in the doorway and watched.

They used their voices, their gestures, and their tone of voice. Sometimes a line from some play would creep in, conveniently carried over for the occasion. I thought that Mama was the worst. Doesn't Papa hear how false it sounds? Doesn't he see how she takes stock of her effect with her left eye while she cries with the right? Doesn't he notice how she controls the game and forces him into the strangest lines?

Mama was in total control of her talent, but she couldn't fool me. One time I said to her: Stop playing a role, Mama, I'm a bad audience. It's not worth the trouble. Then she gave me a look that frightened me and she said: "This is my only means of expression, I have no other. Whether real or unreal. I suffer, I'm alone, try to understand that." (*In another tone of voice*) I never thought how childish Mama was. I didn't realize—

RACHEL walks onto the stage. She stops in the darkness beyond the reach of the ramp lights, stands in uncertainty. ANNA looks at her own hands, absently, indifferently. HENRIK VOGLER looks up and sees RACHEL.

RACHEL It's raining.

VOGLER Oh, it is? Yes, now I hear it.

RACHEL A real autumn rain.

VOGLER Well, it is autumn.

RACHEL Did I catch you napping?

VOGLER No.

RACHEL I'm looking for my shoes; I left them somewhere. So I went out in my rehearsal shoes and now they're sopping wet.

RACHEL sits on a stool in the middle of the stage and changes her shoes. Her skirt slides up over her thighs. She coughs. VOGLER looks at her with distaste.

VOGLER Do you have a cold?

RACHEL Have no fear. I've been dragging around with this cough for four years.

VOGLER You smoke too much.

RACHEL That's it, precisely. I smoke too much.

VOGLER So what other kind of unpleasantness are you dragging in?

RACHEL Can't we go to bed together?

VOGLER Here?

RACHEL In your room, darling. We have actually done it before.

VOGLER You're not sober.

RACHEL So unpleasant.

VOGLER It is unpleasant.

RACHEL Come on, Henrik!

VOGLER I'm not in the mood.

RACHEL You're in the mood. You're in the mood, but it embarrasses you.

She sits facing him, her skirt still high up on her thighs, a shoe on her left foot, her face heavy with drink, her thick hair moist with rain, no makeup on her face.

VOGLER We have nothing—

RACHEL —more to say to one another. Precisely. But we can make love. There's never been any misunderstanding about that, has there, my friend?

VOGLER No.

RACHEL I have looked into your face, deep into it. Into its inner side. We have no secrets from each other.

VOGLER That sounds like a line from a bad play.

RACHEL (*smiles*) One of yours, maybe?

VOGLER Thanks.

Pause.

RACHEL You're a big shit.

VOGLER Here we go.

RACHEL Why do you force me to play a role with only two lines? Can you tell me that? Can you give me one good reason, aside from the fact that it amuses you to humiliate me in front of my colleagues?

VOGLER Do you really *want* to know the truth?

RACHEL Your evasions have always amused me.

VOGLER I'm going to try to control my distaste for exactly one minute in order to explain to you why I wanted you to play Edith's mother in this production.

RACHEL You're getting red under the eyes. That's always been the sign for me.

VOGLER (*tired*) The sign for what?

RACHEL (*friendly*) The sign that one of Henrik's more serious lies is coming up.

VOGLER You really are a plague.

RACHEL A contagious one.

VOGLER (*after a pause*) Almost a year ago I called you and told you about this production. I asked you if you would play Edith's mother for old times' sake. You cried and thanked me and said that I had made you insanely happy, that you were grateful that I hadn't forgotten you, and so on. We spoke for an hour to each other. Later that night you called me again, obviously drunk, and said that you were so insanely grateful and that you still loved me. Now exactly a minute has passed and I have given you my explanation. I could add something else— but we can let that go. It doesn't figure in here.

RACHEL I can just imagine your conversation with the boss: "I was thinking of asking Rachel to play Edith's mother." "Isn't that risky? She's in bad shape right now, she's been on sick leave for three months, I don't know if you'll be able to stand her. She's gotten sloppy and lost her discipline." You sit there

silently for a little while and think about *old* Rachel. You nod
and smile and say that you'll call her: "I'll call Rachel," you
say, "she can decide."

VOGLER Do you still live at home?

RACHEL No.

VOGLER Are you living on your own?

RACHEL You know very well that I'm in the hospital.

VOGLER I didn't know that, actually.

RACHEL (*smiles*) Don't play dumb, darling.

VOGLER I didn't know. Word of honor.

RACHEL For Anna's sake.

VOGLER What about Michael?

RACHEL Michael endures everything, hopes everything, be-
lieves everything. He is nice.(*Affected tone*) Michael is nice.

VOGLER And Anna?

RACHEL Are you interested?

VOGLER Rachel! (*Impatient gesture*)

RACHEL She's fine.

VOGLER That's an exhaustive answer.

RACHEL What am I supposed to say? She's fine.

VOGLER How old is she?

RACHEL She'll turn twelve this June.

VOGLER How are she and Michael getting along?

RACHEL It's a grand love affair. She's like you, by the way.

VOGLER You mean in some unpleasant way.

RACHEL Anna sells people out.

VOGLER I don't get it.

RACHEL To please her father she sells out her mother.

VOGLER Maybe she has her reasons.

RACHEL Of course. We're sitting at the dinner table. Michael is reading something from the newspaper. I ask him to stop reading. He gets up from the table, folds the newspaper, walks up and hits me in the face with it. Then he takes his coat and hat and slams the door on his way out. The next day I overhear a conversation between Anna and Michael. Anna says that she feels sorry for her father, that she doesn't understand how he can stand it any longer. And so on. (*Smiles*)

VOGLER You mean Michael actually hit you? It sounds—

RACHEL Unbelievable.

VOGLER Michael, who's the world's—

RACHEL —nicest, gentlest.

VOGLER Poor Rachel.

RACHEL People can do what they like with me, isn't that so? However they want? Henrik? Isn't that so?

Pause.

VOGLER That's the risky thing about you.

RACHEL I was the best. Wasn't I?

VOGLER Yes, you were the best.

RACHEL For twenty-six years I was the best.

VOGLER If you really wanted, you could still—

RACHEL Thanks. Thanks for the compliment. By the way, can you see that my upper teeth are coming loose?

VOGLER No.

RACHEL I'm rotting, bit by bit. Even when I was twenty years old, playing Margareta. Do you remember the final scene? Even then I knew how the waltzes go. Decay. It was there. It was present.

VOGLER Yes, it was.

RACHEL But you couldn't see it at the time. Do you remember that we had a program with folk songs on the radio? We sang and played. Then there was Strindberg's *Princess Bride*, you were there that time, too.

VOGLER Yes.

RACHEL What's keeping you from sleeping with me? I've had two glasses of red wine, neither more nor less. I'm not drunk, if that's what you think.

VOGLER I don't think anything.

RACHEL My thighs are still as smooth as a young girl's. My body is undamaged. My breasts! Just look. Well, what do you say? Henrik says nothing. He sits there, staring and silent. Henrik is undecided. He's horny but lacks the desire. He's not looking at my thighs or my breasts, he's looking at my face, and my face is——

VOGLER Why are you in the hospital?

RACHEL My kind doctor thought it was for the best.

VOGLER During your episodes.

RACHEL During my episodes.

VOGLER And at other times?

RACHEL I have a little apartment on the courtyard behind the theater. It's a beautiful old courtyard with a big chestnut tree right outside my window. In the summer the light in my room turns green, like in an aquarium. Come, let's go to my place. Five minutes. Four minutes.

VOGLER No. I'm waiting for somebody.

RACHEL That little doctor of mine is thoughtful, believe you me. We have long conversations, they call it conversation therapy. He talks about himself and then he fucks me afterward. A little, dry, helpless fucker, he takes it slow, his hands are cold and sweaty. You're waiting for somebody, you say.

That's remarkable. You've never waited for anyone before, I'll bet. Who is the awaited one?

VOGLER That doesn't concern you.

RACHEL You're probably right. So my doctor calls Michael, and my husband and my doctor talk about Rachel and her condition, while Rachel lies on the floor of her little white room and masturbates.

VOGLER It probably hasn't occurred to you that your husband and the doctor mean well.

RACHEL I am completely convinced that the two of them are completely convinced that they mean well.

VOGLER Can't you get a new doctor?

RACHEL And what would that accomplish? I get the care I need. I've been given the run of a white cubicle where I can house my screams, my prayers, my vomit, and my despair. I am privileged, as they say, and I am boundlessly grateful.

VOGLER You actually look better than the last time we met. That was—let me see—two years ago.

RACHEL Will I never be able to play a major role again?

VOGLER That depends on you.

RACHEL Cut the crap, Henrik! I am asking you straight out whether I will ever again play a major role. Has my fear gotten too great? Will I die of despair? Will I throw up on stage, have an attack of diarrhea—shit my pants? Did you know that I have a plastic bucket behind the curtain? What will I do with myself? Whether I'm working or "resting," as they say, my despair is just as great. I take sedatives, I get injections. My despair is below the surface, I feel it all the time, like a toothache that's been numbed. Do you think that my instrument has been destroyed for all time? In that case, I will have to die. That's just hot air, by the way, I don't want to die at all, I'm afraid to die, I can't imagine that I would seriously injure myself. Do you think that my instrument has been ruined?

VOGLER Actually, I don't.

RACHEL I told them time after time, don't do it, don't do it—it will be a deadly catastrophe. I know that it is a deadly catastrophe.

VOGLER I don't know what you're talking about.

RACHEL It was a completely ordinary argument between Michael and me. I knew that he was lying. I tried to get him to tell the truth. *Just that one time.* But it was fruitless. He lied and he held on to that lie. He reduced my mind to rubble. Do you understand what that means? By lying he poisoned and tore apart my mind. He raped my instincts. I *know* that I behaved badly. I *know* that I screamed and cried and locked myself into the bathroom. I hit Anna, who had begun to shriek. First I tried to comfort her, but she didn't want to be comforted, she tore herself away from me and rushed to Michael for protection, then I hit her. I regret that, I have regretted that every day. Michael called our friend the doctor, and so he came, along with a locksmith and police and men in white coats and I got a shot. I fought them with all my strength, but they held me tight and gave me a shot so that I faded away. I just wanted Michael to tell the truth for once. I wanted to hear the truth no matter how repulsive it was. I can't live with the lies, my reality gets unreal, I lose my balance.

VOGLER Normal people can't live up to your demand for truth.

RACHEL (*laughs*) You couldn't, either.

VOGLER It's fine onstage, but not in my private life, thank you.

RACHEL Hasn't Michael told you about it? Hasn't the boss? Or someone else?

VOGLER I didn't know about this. (*He raises his hand in denial.*)

RACHEL (*after a long pause*) You were involved, too.

VOGLER On my word of honor, no.

RACHEL Michael called you. You were abroad somewhere. He asked you to try to talk to me.

VOGLER (*tired*) That's not true.

RACHEL You advised Michael to call the hospital and the police. It was *you* who said that there was a risk I would commit suicide, even though you knew that I have never seriously tried to hurt myself.

VOGLER Stop trying to provoke me, if you please.

RACHEL You and Michael and Dr. Jacobi. (*Laughs softly*)

VOGLER Your conspiracy theory is a complete fantasy. I knew nothing.

RACHEL Each of you on your own couldn't beat me down, not even two of you ganging up could, but all three of you together were sufficiently clever. I admit that you had serious enough reasons.

VOGLER What reasons are you talking about? We had been your lovers and you brought us up between your knees and then you threw us aside and went for new victims. Even back when you were with me you drank pretty heavily and when you were drunk you were hard on me and hard on yourself. (*He makes a sound mixed with impatience, disgust, and rage.*)

RACHEL Good God, help me. Help me. "The sea is so great and my boat is so little. I am a believer without a God. Without religion, without hope. Cruelty, infatuation, conformity, the merciless conformity to routine, eternally, to the end of time."

(*Affected*) Why can't you take just one more chance on me? I promise you, you won't be disappointed.

VOGLER I don't dare to.

RACHEL What a stupid answer! Didn't you just say yourself that I'm still a magnificent instrument? You can hear notes sound through me that have never been heard before. Isn't that worth an experiment? (*She sits on the chair in the middle of the stage and recites.*) "My own mother's sister in her blindness has *denied* the divine origin of Dionysus. That is why I have stung them with this madness that drives them, raging like madwomen, from house and home. With the emblem of the orgy I have forced every woman of the tribe of Kadmos to take to the mountains. Around the daughters of Kadmos they gather, out in the wilderness among the cliffs and the forest of firs, ever green. Yes, this city, where the cry of Bacchus has never sounded, will expiate the sin of humiliating my mother and, willingly or not, will do penance."

VOGLER Yes.

Pause.

RACHEL Are you in such despair about your own tumult that you can't deal with the unpredictable?

VOGLER You're beginning to get unbearably theatrical.

RACHEL Oh, am I? (*Little laugh*) Sorry.

VOGLER I administrate, communicate, organize the unsayable, the terrifying, the dangerous. I don't take part in the drama, I materialize it. I despise the spontaneous, the unconsidered, the imprecise. I am here in order to enable you to fix your inspiration in such a way that it will give the audience the impression of an inspiration. I have no room for my own complications, other than as keys to the secrets of the text or as impulses for the actors' creativity. I hate tumult, aggressions, outbursts. My rehearsal is an operation in an operating room. Here self-discipline, purity, light, and quiet rule. A rehearsal is a rigorous task, not private therapy for directors and actors. I disdain Walter, who comes in drunk and vomits up his private complications at ten-thirty in the morning. I'm disgusted by Teresa, who runs up and hugs me and kisses me in a cloud of sweat and bad perfume. I'd like to torture Paul, who shows up in shoes with high heels, despite the fact that he knows that he has to run up and down stairs on the stage all day. I despise Vanya, who rushes in a minute late, his hair on end, unwashed and panting, loaded down with bags. I want quiet, order, and kindness. *That's* the only way for us to approach the boundlessness, the difficulties, the darkness. *That's* the only way we can solve the riddles and learn the mechanism of repetition. I take care of texts and rehearsal times. I am responsible for keeping your work from being meaningless. I am not private, I observe, register, control. I suggest, tempt, encourage, or say no. I am not spontaneous, impulsive, part of the action. It only looks that way. If for one second I were to tear off my mask and say what I felt or thought, you would all turn on me in a rage, tear me apart, and throw me out the window.

RACHEL (*kindly*) Idiot. Theater is shit and squalor and horniness and tumult, confusion and the blackest kind of mischief. I don't believe your purity theory at all. It is false and highly suspect. Just like you.

VOGLER How would it be if—no, never mind, it's not worth it. And I can't understand why I don't—

RACHEL Why not. I am the world's most gullible person.

VOGLER Sure.

RACHEL As many lies as you and others of your ilk have fed me through the years, it's lucky that I'm not only gullible, but forgetful, too.

VOGLER (*retreating*) Right. It's a good thing.

RACHEL Why so bored?

VOGLER I'm not bored at all. I'm just wondering how many victims pave—

RACHEL (*laughs, then*) Here I am in my beloved theater, fortysix years old. My former lover has deigned to give me two lines in his play. I offer myself to him and he can't even be bothered to fuck me behind those sets over there, because I'm drunk or maybe only tipsy. He thinks I'm ugly and disgusting. He thinks that my face—my face—(*almost crying*) I stink like a rotten fish, some fluid is oozing from my skin that smells like carrion. My makeup won't even stay on anymore, it runs into my wrinkles, bunches up in little grains. I breathe decay, I know that, do you think I don't know? I try to keep my nails clean but they split and turn black. Jesus. (*Laughs*) And you talk about "victims paving my road to success."

VOGLER My dear Rachel, that was a compliment.

RACHEL Oh, I see, a compliment. (*Blows her nose*) Excuse me. I know that you despise my tears, I know that you're disgusted by me blowing my nose into a dirty handkerchief, but I don't have another one and I got oil on my hands when I—(*cries*)

VOGLER (*almost tenderly*) I absolutely do not want to hurt you. Do you hear what I'm saying? (*She nods, blows her nose.*) Rachel?

RACHEL If you don't dare to put on something serious, we could do a comedy together. You know that I'm a first-class co-median. I've never played Strindberg's Kristina. Wouldn't it be fun to do Kristina? Am I too old for *Pygmalion*? Or Feydeau? There must be a funny Feydeau we could do? Molière? I would make a good Dorine. She really doesn't have to be especially young. The French always make her into an old bitch, but I think that's wrong because her breasts are supposed to be— she always shows a lot of cleavage, and I—there's nothing wrong with my figure, just my face. I'll play Dorine, there's no risk there, and Michael will do Orgon and Ernst Tartuffe. Wouldn't that be fun?

VOGLER I've never had a success with *Tartuffe*.

RACHEL That's why you need to try it one more time.

VOGLER Actually, I think the play is boring.

RACHEL (*sadly*) I see.

VOGLER That's what I've always thought.

RACHEL Then I guess it's not such a great idea.

VOGLER No.

RACHEL I'll be going now.

VOGLER Stay, if you like.

RACHEL No, I'm going. I'm just disturbing you.

VOGLER No, no, you're not disturbing me in the slightest.

RACHEL Besides, you said you were waiting for someone.

VOGLER I just said that.

RACHEL You were upset that I came to see you.

VOGLER (*leans forward*) Rachel. You never believe what I say, but try to believe this: There's not a day that goes by that I don't think of you. Every night before my sleeping pill knocks me out, I think of you. You are always in my thoughts. That's the way it is, Rachel.

RACHEL (*affected*)How nice of you to say that.

VOGLER It's not nice, it's the truth.

RACHEL I mean that it was nice of you to tell me.

VOGLER Go back to your apartment and clean up the worst of the mess, and I'll be there in an hour.

RACHEL You're just saying that to get rid of me. All right, all right, I'm going. (*Gestures*) I'm going. Maybe you'd even be interested in some dinner? Should I make us something good? Like the old days.

VOGLER No, thanks. Don't go to any trouble.

RACHEL It's no trouble. That's Henrik Vogler: Don't go to any trouble for my sake. Don't be angry, Henrik. I have to be able to joke with you a little. Or is that forbidden now.

VOGLER You have the upper hand. As usual.

RACHEL When you come, you'll find me bathed, sweet-smelling, and sober. The great unconscious. (*She stretches her arms above her head, knits her fingers.*) Oh, Henrik, my beloved friend. Do you think I would have been happier in life if I had learned to be cynical?

VOGLER I am definitely coming. Now go.

She kisses him and quickly departs.

VOGLER (*calls softly*) Rachel!

But she doesn't answer, she is gone. ANNA sits as before, with her head slightly bowed. She looks at her hands, a quick and affirming smile crosses her face.

ANNA It's true. I am childish for my age. Sometimes it's almost embarrassing. Gullible, sloppy, and naïve.

VOGLER In our profession, childishness is rather common. How in the hell do you think it could be otherwise? Sometimes it astonishes me that anyone takes us seriously at all. That people build great halls for us, where we can get together and play our games. Protect your childishness. It is your only defense against awareness, which in your case is almost palpable.

ANNA When I'm in the grip of passion, I'm not aware at all.

VOGLER Falling in love. Jealousy. Are you a jealous person?

ANNA About normal.

VOGLER Oh, I see. Normal. That sounds reassuring, but hardly truthful. No, yes—I believe you.

ANNA And what about you?

VOGLER Hardly normal.

ANNA You're looking at me and definitely thinking of saying something astonishing, and then I think: Is this Uncle Henrik's way of courting young ladies?

VOGLER That wasn't nice.

ANNA I'm in love with you, of course.

VOGLER Aha, is that how it is?

ANNA Did I ruin what you were thinking of saying to me?

VOGLER If it makes you happy I am certainly able to say that I have a weakness for you, that I'm in love, if you like. I am happy that you exist, that you're sitting here beside me on the *Hedda Gabler* sofa. That I can reach you with my hand. I am happy that we have at least five weeks of work before us, that you are tied to me professionally and therefore emotionally. I am in love with you because you are a beautiful young person, because you are a uniquely talented person, and not least of all because you are a good actress. (*Sits, gray*)

ANNA (*after a pause*) All of that was beautifully said, and I will remember this moment for the rest of my life.

VOGLER Of course I'm jealous. That's a part of it. I know that you're living with that little walleyed assistant director, whatever his name is, Peter something. He is not only unusually badly brought up, he also completely lacks talent, at least if one is to judge from the Brecht play he put on up at the Studio. That he was able, for some incomprehensible reason, to attach himself to you has to be regarded as a triumph of mediocrity. But perhaps he has characteristics invisible to the rest of the world, what do I know? What does your Papa say about the relationship?

ANNA He thinks that Peter is sweet.

VOGLER Oh. Sweet. Are you sure that he didn't say it ironically? "Peter is a sweet lad," or something like that?

ANNA Peter and I are expecting a child.

VOGLER I knew it. How far along are you? Two months?

ANNA Three.

VOGLER I knew it. It's just too ridiculous.

ANNA What is ridiculous?

VOGLER You'll be almost five months along by the time we get to opening night. How long will you be able to act? Three weeks? Fourteen days? Our work takes on new meaning this way. Forgive my irritation. But—

ANNA (*interrupting*) So now you are no longer happy about our work together.

VOGLER (*gray*) I don't understand a thing. A young, ambitious actress is offered the world's best role. It is a decisive moment in her career and she has known for over a year that she is scheduled to play this role now. She gets pregnant. I don't understand it.

ANNA So you're no longer in love?

VOGLER No, on the contrary. (*He sits silently, runs his hand over the worn fabric of the sofa again and again.*)

ANNA (*after a pause*) What do you mean?

VOGLER What is a dramatic production, anyway. One big, orderly tumult. We concern ourselves with the issues, with considerable spiritual exertion. It is almost a matter of life and death. Then the opening night comes and it is very exciting. The director falls away, he is transformed into an appendix. The play runs for thirty, sixty, a hundred performances. Then we strike it and it's gone. Everything is forgotten, in most cases it's a mercy. To direct you as Agnes in *The Dream Play* is fun. That the production will be done after two weeks makes it even more fun. It won't be a play, it will be a child, probably something much more meaningful. If I think about it properly, it's magnificent, except that of course I'm even angrier at that assistant director you're hanging out with, whatever his name is. It must feel like a real triumph for him that he managed to squelch my *Dream Play*.

ANNA Would you want me to have an abortion?

VOGLER No. (*Pause*) No. Not for the theater. It's not worth it.

ANNA But you just said—

VOGLER Don't mind what I happened to say five minutes ago, it was the old man of the theater talking, the one who has to be convinced that his efforts are worthwhile. Don't mind him, I'm tired of him myself.

ANNA I'll talk to the boss tomorrow.

VOGLER And give up the role.

ANNA Yes.

VOGLER And who will take your place?

ANNA There are several who could.

VOGLER Nobody I want. You were the idea behind this production. You were the very—

ANNA I've said what I wanted to say.

VOGLER —and what about your watch?

ANNA That was just a bad excuse.

VOGLER I don't want you to give up the role.

ANNA What about your aggression? How will I be able to stand it? Can you tell me that?

VOGLER I already told you that—(*Falls silent*)

ANNA There won't be any child.

VOGLER (*looking at her*) Have you already had an abortion?

ANNA Last week. I said that I was—

VOGLER You did away with the child.

ANNA I want to play my role.

VOGLER I understand.

ANNA My relationship to Peter is practically dead. It is just so hard to—

VOGLER I see.

ANNA This summer I'm going to make a film and Peter will be traveling abroad. Then everything will be simpler. I mean the divorce.

VOGLER What did you say?

ANNA I don't know. It just occurred to me.

VOGLER Did you want to see how I would react?

ANNA Is that so wrong? I wanted to see you lose your face.

VOGLER (*tired*) And—

ANNA And you did. You lost your face.

VOGLER Well, then, you got your money's worth out of your little joke.

ANNA Now I'm going to wipe away that sad face. (*She runs her right hand over his face.*)

VOGLER (*immobile*) No.

Anna kisses him suddenly on the mouth.

VOGLER Sometimes you remind me of your mother.

ANNA (*smiling*) I'm sad that I've made you sad. I don't know what to do with myself.

VOGLER (*mildly*) I don't like it when you put on an act.

ANNA (*pulls back*) Are you so sure that you know how to interpret any reaction? Aren't you ever wrong?

VOGLER Not with you.

ANNA I wasn't putting on an act.

VOGLER You made a tender gesture. In fact, you wanted to hit me.

ANNA That's not true.

VOGLER You are a lot like your mother.

ANNA If you say one more time that I am like my mother, if you say one more time that I—I'm leaving.

VOGLER You are a lot like your mother.

They look at each other.

ANNA I'm going to tell you something that will astonish you.

VOGLER Now I'm really curious.

ANNA Peter admires you. Now you're surprised.

VOGLER Now I am surprised.

ANNA He would have been happy to be your assistant on *The Dream Play* and was enormously disappointed when he found out that you had asked for Eva instead.

VOGLER I really thought that—

ANNA Peter thinks that you are the only one who has something to teach. He was glad that I was going to get to work with you. He was glad and jealous at the same time.

VOGLER And then you got pregnant.

ANNA I wanted the baby. He was the one who convinced me to have the abortion. Now you're surprised again.

VOGLER I guess I am.

ANNA I wanted the baby, even though it wasn't Peter's and even though I wouldn't get to act in your production. I was afraid that I would never get pregnant again if I—but Peter convinced me. So now here I am. In your hands. (*Smiles*)

VOGLER And I in yours. (*Immobile*) I have lived alone for eight years. An old lady visits me for three hours every day. She cleans and fixes my supper, does the dishes, and disappears. I have a few friends. We talk about politics and play chess. My wife visits me sometimes, when she's in the mood. We spend the evening and the night together, we are rather attached to one another.

ANNA I'll only come when you call me.

VOGLER Your mother also had the most fantastic notions about how she should relate to life and reality. They were never quite in tune.

ANNA My mother was a hysteric.

VOGLER And you're not. (*He looks at her.*) All the red lights are flashing and the warning signals are buzzing. I ought to get up and leave. I ought to say, now it's about time for an elderly gentleman to take his afternoon nap and have his afternoon whiskey. An evil psychologist has said that the temperature of a passion can only be measured in relation to the loneliness that precedes it. I don't know. I had imagined this differently. We would have our work, our rehearsals, our hours on the stage. *The Dream Play* and us.

ANNA (*suddenly*) So annoying that I destroyed your plans.

VOGLER I'm just offering my experience. Be my guest. I'll give you empathy, consideration, and tenderness from ten-thirty to three. I'll see to it that the audience loves you, that you'll have lighting that highlights your beauty. I'll protect you from yourself, I'll take you by the hand and make sure you don't fall. Between ten-thirty and three. You mustn't touch me. (*Pause*) I am uninteresting. I'm all played out. Someone sat down and wrote my role, gave himself pains to do it, but the role never came to life. I am a tiresome character. Played out and nearly finished. I'm telling you that without the least hint of flirtation. I refuse to play in your drama. It would only be ridiculous and humiliating. No, of course not. (*Gestures*) Not for you. What did you think would come of it, anyway? A drama of passion, a love story, or just playacting on overtime? You have an extraordinarily competent father, do you really need another one? Is it the beginning of my decay that attracts you? My ugly, deformed, unwilling body? That can't be possible, in any case. Just before we began our rehearsals, I lost a front tooth. I was in a cold sweat of despair. Do I have to appear before Anna Egerman with a gap in my upper teeth? She won't listen to me, she'll find me repulsive. Look at this tooth here, it's artificial, can you see that? A gifted dentist took pity on me and worked a miracle. I was able to appear with my authority and teeth intact.

It's undeniably true that you attract me. I want to hold you in my arms, caress you, kiss you, sleep with you. Nothing about you is strange or repellent. In my current predicament it would be good to find something repellent, even something very minor, something to make much of and blow out of proportion, something that could be of use. But there's nothing like that in you. I am left to my own devices, helpless.

(*Silence*)

I have told myself time after time that you are much too much like your mother, that this is the very reason I have to be careful. I believe that you can be cruel without consideration for your victim. I believe that you can lie rather cleverly, not to win an advantage but in order to manipulate. I believe that you have a place for me in your plan. Maybe our affair would improve your relationship with Peter. I don't know. Maybe I'm being unfair.

ANNA Now there's much more to say.

VOGLER Sure there is. You could tell me I'm wrong.

ANNA Would I be able to convince you? Do you even want to be convinced? Would it pay to protest? If I say that your analysis is correct, how will that help me? How can it help us?

VOGLER Don't take it so seriously. Only theater critics believe in objective truth, even while they're teasing us by asserting the opposite.

ANNA Put your hand on my breast.

VOGLER is well on the way, but stops himself at the last moment.

VOGLER No, no. (*Pause*) No. No, thank you.

ANNA (*smiles*) Thank you, no?

VOGLER "If only I were ten years younger." No, what a line! Lines like that ought to be outlawed.

ANNA (*laughs*) You don't make a very convincing defense.

VOGLER If only I were ten years younger. After the first week, we started talking to each other after the rehearsals. We had to discuss your role, right? Come on, let's get a cup of coffee in the cafeteria. Some carefully chosen colleague goes along as our alibi. Then we start to meet in my room. We sit far apart and drink mineral water and eat something sweet, but not too sweet. When you leave, we kiss each other on the mouth. One day we talk about the difficulties in your love life. You sell me Peter and I buy your package. One day you arrive at rehearsal in a deep depression and weepy-eyed. When I ask what's happened, you just shake your head. That day we work wonderfully together. At three I go up to you and ask if you want to have dinner with me at seven. You look at me with sad honesty and nod. Then you arrive fifteen minutes too late, right? We eat dinner, drink wine, and talk about you all evening. I become more and more inspired and explain you to yourself. We're madly in love with ourselves, with the whole situation, with the play that's going so marvelously. At eleven I drive you home. Our relationship is delicious and full of promise. I kiss you on the cheek and tell you to take care of yourself. You look at me with a mysterious smile and slowly shake your head. Your eyes, your very beautiful eyes, fill with tears. And so you leave me without a word. Several evenings later we go to bed with each other for the first time, more playful than anything else. Like a first attempt, a test that didn't count. The experience leaves behind a sweet and arousing sense of lack of satisfaction, an experience that awakens curiosity.

Now three weeks of rehearsals have passed. You live with me and you live with Peter—you can't stand to hurt him. We move into a heavier and deeper sensual bliss. At the same time, the temperature at work rises. An old actor slaps me on the shoulder and says "You haven't changed a bit since the days of your youth." He gives me a shameless grin. I'm terribly flattered and immediately decide to consider him talented but misunderstood. Peter lurks around in the corners, receiving the attentions of pitying young female theater students. The mood is a general euphoria, broken now and then by violent but harmless thunderstorms. We have begun to meet regularly, mostly in the afternoons between the rehearsal and the performance. I spend the evenings alone at a movie theater or in my hotel. In the early mornings I fall prey to insane jealousy: I see the most mundane images of you with Peter. I foam at the mouth and cry, but at ten-fifteen we meet on the stage with a smile and a quick, collegial kiss. Then, when just four weeks of rehearsal are left, the crisis comes. You've been rehearsing for five weeks, happy, flattered, in a glow of pleasant feelings. The crisis comes when you have to sober up professionally. Your self-criticism and your lack of self-confidence pounce on you like raging tigers. You think you are bad, needy, bottled-up, maudlin. The worst of it is that I think exactly the same thing. The only difference is that you can say what you feel, while I am forced to lie. We have also committed the banal stupidity of beginning to talk about the future. We plan a trip abroad for your vacation. I also start trying to think of a good film role for you, and have already told "everything" in strictest confidence to my old friend the producer, that jerk. He lays his hand over mine, leans forward, looks into my eyes, and says: "How wonderful for you and how wonderful for the girl. What kind of budget did you have in mind?" One day you and I fall into an argument during a rehearsal. What do you think we're fighting about? It must be something small.

ANNA During four rehearsals I have tripped up at the same place in the text, because I think that I am especially bad at that particular place. You get irritated and—

VOGLER —say: "How would it be if you took a look at that line some afternoon."

ANNA That would be completely meaningless, since I have never understood what it says there.

VOGLER I have, in fact, explained to you a number of times—

ANNA I'm probably stupid, but your explanations have only made that passage even more mysterious.

VOGLER Then I suggest that you read the text carefully and read it in a loud and clear voice so that the audience hears what you say. That is a good, simple method, when an actor persists in not *wanting* to understand.

ANNA So you believe I'm being stubborn.

VOGLER I believe absolutely nothing: "And moreover I think that there is not the slightest reason for tears. We'll go on with the next scene so that Anna has time to collect herself, blow her nose, wash her face, and cheer up."

ANNA When we meet later at the hotel, you ask my forgiveness and you're wonderful and loving and—

VOGLER Not at all. On the contrary. The jealousy I've repressed for five weeks now comes out in an intolerable scene in which I hear myself mouth all the idiocies I solemnly swore to myself that I'd never—

ANNA Now it turns out that I am much more jealous than you, and I begin to rage about your beautiful, tolerant, and charming wife who has just been for a visit. You didn't know that I knew, and you are caught with no answer.

VOGLER You must not know me very well. I am not caught without an answer at all, but offer to end our affair and grant you free passage. I maintain that I'm too old for your childish squabbling and from then on wrap myself in a melancholy silence. That makes you uncertain; you've lost your exit lines. For the first time you see that I am bleary-eyed, old, and a little ridiculous. You're just about to finish me off and raise your knife to cut me down when you stop yourself.

ANNA Suddenly I see that there is something moving about you. I am seized with maternal feelings.

VOGLER You're not seized with maternal feelings at all. Instead you start thinking about your role. "How will he act if we tear our relationship apart? Will he want revenge, maybe? What will my friends say! They'll get a real kick out of this!" You don't want to grant your friends that pleasure. "First we'll have opening night, and then we'll call it quits. That's how it will be." You drop the deadly dagger and begin to cry. I misunderstand your tears and try to comfort you. We end up in bed, illusory reconciliation, and so on.

ANNA (*smiles*) Now you're just being mean.

VOGLER The sixth week of rehearsals passes under a guarded silence. You have a magnificent cold. I keep my distance because of my germ phobia. You think I'm a coward and despise me. Peter, who is now in the lead, takes care of you, fixes you warm drinks, and starts to plan your vacation together.

ANNA (*forceful*) You and your actresses!

VOGLER Now there are only three weeks of rehearsals left. We have made up, but only on the surface. That gives our relationship a new taste, both bitter and intense, but far from unpleasant. We begin to glimpse our true faces behind the masks. It's exciting, and we spur each other on. We don't talk so much about the future, which utterly compromises our present. We feel disgust and sorrow. The last week is harrowing. We try to excuse ourselves. Neither of us listens to the other, our conversations are nothing more than despairing monologues. The temperature rises. We move into dress rehearsal. Lighting, costumes, makeup.

ANNA I feel disgusting and inadequate. I want to be the Daughter of Indra that you'll never forget. The one that would make it impossible for you to ever do *The Dream Play* again. I realize that you're already secretly planning a new production with another star. I cry often. You are tender and considerate and treat me as if I had been stricken with a deadly disease. At the same time, you distance yourself.

VOGLER I have to distance myself from you and I must distance myself from the production. I go through the same hell every time.

ANNA And so we come to our last evening together. It's the evening after the dress rehearsal. We drink a few glasses of wine and our senses intoxicate us. We hear ourselves talking of the future, other productions together, we make plans.

VOGLER We talk about how maybe we should get married, that it would be fun to have children together. We recall marriages we know that have lasted a long time. Everything is sad and pretty much over, something we both know with a painful clarity.

ANNA (*pause*) Did I ever get that film role you promised me?

VOGLER No, my friend the producer cheated me out of the money and you got a better offer.

ANNA And when we meet?

VOGLER It's friendly. Peter's a part of it, too. We eat together as a threesome and talk about the miserable state of the theater. (*Laughs, falls silent*) That's how it would have been.

ANNA (*after a silence*) Was it so crazy, then?

VOGLER (*laughs*) No. (*Pause*) No. Not at all.

Long silence, both of them lost in thought. VOGLER has taken ANNA's hand and holds it. She carefully frees herself, gets up, and walks toward the darkness of the stage. Far away, as if from another world, the ringing of bells and ambulance sirens can be heard.

ANNA This conversation made me sad.

VOGLER Is that right?

ANNA You don't see me. Do you see me?

VOGLER I think I do.

ANNA I forgot about my rehearsal for the radio. I should have been there at three-thirty. How careless of me!

VOGLER Blame it on me. Say that Vogler made you stay after. Everyone will understand and feel sorry for you.

ANNA That might work. I'll call right away.

VOGLER Do that. I'll sit here a little while longer.

ANNA Can you hear the church bells?

VOGLER No. My hearing has started to go. Haven't you noticed that at rehearsals?

ANNA Maybe a little. No, actually, I haven't.

VOGLER Go call now.

ANNA I don't want you to be sad.

VOGLER My sadness has nothing to do with you.

ANNA Are you sure?

VOGLER Sure.

ANNA Then I guess I'll go and call, even though it's terribly embarrassing. Are you sure that I can blame you?

VOGLER You can blame me.

ANNA has been standing indecisively far off downstage. She seems about to say something else, but only shakes her head and then walks farther into the shadows. She disappears; her footsteps can no longer be heard. The stage door sighs. VOGLER moves from the sofa to the armchair. He is gray. He pages absentmindedly through the script. The bells have fallen silent.

THE LAST SCREAM
—A SLIGHTLY SKEWED MORALITY TALE

The lovers' tryst that is about to take place has its origins in a discovery I made, quite on my own, of the cinematography of Georg af Klercker. I was familiar with his name, but not his work. Upon further investigation I came upon an enigma: in the brief space of three springs and summers, this man managed to produce twenty-five films! Then he disappears from the world of flickering shadows, only to turn up much later with a real failure. Then it's over. There is something intensely stimulating about this enigma. Because two summers ago I wrote a play. It turned out to be fastidious and terribly conscientious, weighted down with verified facts and relatively accurately drawn characters. Boring and tiresome. Last summer I threw it all out and I wrote *The Last Scream* at a good clip, ignoring completely all possible facts and setting aside objective truth. This was a completely different story, one that I hope is more entertaining and much more truthful, or so I tell myself.

I think that Georg af Klercker is remarkably remarkable. I wonder what images he would have given us had he been allowed to continue and not been broken off at forty years of age.

Even the great ones made tolerable melodramas—we ought to keep that in mind.

Characters

CHARLES MAGNUSSON Powerful film producer

GEORG AF KLERCKER Former lieutenant, film director

ELISABETH HOLM The powerful man's secretary

It is December of 1919. The scene is the producer's office of the newly founded grand enterprise Svensk Filmindustri. The producer himself, CHARLES MAGNUSSON, sits at his desk of gleaming dark wood and studies an account sheet hidden in a brown cover. He is forty-one. Slender, dapper, extraordinarily pale, and very astigmatic behind his dramatically thick glasses. His secretary, MISS HOLM, a tall, stately lady, impeccably dressed, materializes without a sound. *

MISS HOLM Lieutenant af Klercker is waiting.

CHARLES MAGNUSSON How does he look?

MISS HOLM Not bad. Presentable enough. But he doesn't seem quite sober. Would you like for me to—

CHARLES MAGNUSSON No, no, that's all right. Ask him to step in. How long has he been waiting? Almost an hour, I should think.

---

*Translator's note: *The Last Scream* deals with actual historical figures, though they are represented, as Bergman himself points out, in a fictional situation. Charles Magnusson moved from working in independent studios to acting as first head of the corporate Svensk Filmindustri (Swedish Film Industry). One of his financial backers, Ivan Krueger, made his fortune in match manufacture. Georg af Klercker was the director of the films he mentions in the play and many others of the rich Swedish silent era, most of them lost. Victor Seastrom, born Victor Sjöström (1879–1960) and Mauritz Stiller (1873–1928) were internationally renowned directors who had their start in Swedish silent film. Both Seastrom and Stiller worked for a time in Hollywood during the 1920s. Readers may remember Seastrom from his superb performance as an elderly professor in Bergman's *Wild Strawberries* (1957).

MISS HOLM Should I interrupt you at any particular time?

CHARLES MAGNUSSON I'll be going to lunch after I meet with Klercker and will be back by two. It won't be necessary. Thanks.

MISS HOLM Might I go to the dentist at four?

CHARLES MAGNUSSON Naturally, Miss Holm. By all means, go to the dentist! And by the way, you can take this statement of accounts to copy. I'll need it early tomorrow morning for the cinema owner's meeting.

MISS HOLM Of course, Mr. Magnusson.

MISS HOLM takes the dossier and dematerializes. At the same instant, Lieutenant GEORG AF KLERCKER, forty years of age, appears. At some point he must certainly have been a fine figure of a man. His hair and mustache are well groomed and tastefully dyed. He has grown somewhat flabby, but is firmly corseted, a trifle drunk, but it is almost unnoticeable. MAGNUSSON has risen and takes a few steps toward his guest. A somewhat forced embrace.

GEORG AF KLERCKER Hello there, Charlie. Great to see you again at last, you old goat!

CHARLES MAGNUSSON Sit down, Georg, have a seat. Can I offer you anything? A little whiskey, maybe? A cigar? Or what would you say to a cup of coffee?

GEORG AF KLERCKER What's this? Charlie's opening the bar at ten-thirty in the morning? The end must be near! Well, I won't turn you down. And a cigar would just top it off. "If we are born for pleasure, let us take it," as Peer Gynt so fittingly put it. Is this the liquor cabinet? Not bad, my friend. No, no, don't bother to get up, I can serve myself. Would you like anything? No, I thought not. Good Lord, what a classy place you've got here, Charlie old friend! Persian rugs, by God, and that must be a Bonnard. It is a Bonnard, right? Oh, no? Well there's no way to tell. But the furnishings are superb. It must have cost an arm and a leg. You bet. Everything is new and big. Big movie

theaters, big studios, big offices, big artists. Big money. And
that secretary isn't too shabby. She reeks of class. Have you put
it to her yet, old Charlie? Huh? Tell your old buddy Georgie.
You little devil (*laughs, takes a drink*). I'll be damned. It's just
too strange to see you here in all your glory. I can't stop thinking of how we started out, back there in the sticks. We'll never
have that much fun again! Right, Charlie? I remember everything just like yesterday—(*laughs*). Jesus. Do you remember
Death Rides under the Big Tent? Hell, yes, of course you remember that first little miscarriage of your genius. There you
stood with the script in hand, on the verge of bawling. Oh yes,
there were tears in your eyes. Both Victor and Maurie had read
it and said that they wouldn't have anything to do with such a
piece of crap, that's right, that's right, they were full of themselves even back then, but no one could figure out why. And so
I took the script and read it right there, while you blew your
nose into your fine linen handkerchief. And then I said "This
story is *good*, Charlie, cheer up. I'll direct it." Then I asked Victor if he wanted to play the lieutenant's father, but he said no.
He was pissed off because I was going to direct. How could I
direct—I was just the head of the studio, that's what that modest, hypocritical little shit was thinking, and so I played the father myself! (*Laughs*) Oh God, Charlie, what a disaster! But
Calle Barcklind was good. And Selma! Just think how beautiful
and seductive and happy and sweet she was. And she was over
forty! But she still had enough to go around, right, Charlie?
She was the cast pussy—I mean (*laughs*) cast Muse, of course.
Oh, God. (*Pause*) Well it turned into a fine little film, lots of
good reviews, especially in Denmark, you remember, right?
But Selma's thing for crazy hats was a disaster even back
then—do you remember that burial mound she used to wear,
with the four antennae on top and the little feathers fluttering in
the breeze? I begged and pleaded, but it was no use. "Victor
gave it to me," she said, "and it suits me." Yeah, right. Well, so
it goes. Victor hit it big after that, *unbelievably* big with *Terje*

Vigen. Who would have thought that the aristocratic old maid
had it in him? Hell, no, I'm not bitter, no, no, not in the slightest. I don't begrudge him his incomprehensible success. But if
I'm honest, I'd have to say that I have never seen anything
more deplorable than his *Berg-Eyvind*. Though you have to
admit, Edith is a real piece in that. I wouldn't say no if she offered. Hell no, I'm not pissed off at Victor, not in the slightest.
Though he did scheme to get me out of the Lidingö studio and
went around behind my back, spreading shit about me and trying to get Selma between the sheets. (*Pause*) Jesus, Charlie!
Time has just run away from us and our movies. You've made
it, you're at the top, the biggest and strongest of them all. Now
that Ivan Krueger has put—what was it—five million into
your pretty little company. And here I sit breathing in the scent
of good leather furniture, drinking your fine whiskey and
smoking your elegant cigars, and I have the honor of gazing
upon you, though I can hardly tell if you're gazing back from
behind those pop-bottle glasses of yours, and to be honest,
you're looking more washed-out than ever—but that's how it
is when you make it in this blood-and-guts butchery business.
Here I sit with you, Charlie-boy, and I guess I'm little better
than a beggar. I haven't made a film in more than a year; the last
one was *The Lighthouse Keeper's Daughter*, which I made in the
summer of '17, and now it's—well, a long time ago now. I was
a little curious about why you haven't been in touch. I did
make twenty-five films in three years, you'll recall, and most of
them were box-office successes, too. Maybe the reviews
weren't always the best. (*Laughs*) But Jesus, that's what you
expect. The worst ones were for *Love's Victory*, when they
blasted Selma's clothes. Well, yeah, she was an absolute fright,
I have to agree. But I didn't stand a chance. This is how it was,
Charlie—I can't prove a thing, but I am convinced that this is
how it went: Selma took a trip down to Stockholm to shop for
clothes. I was all tied up with that damned mother-in-law comedy. So she runs into Maurie Stiller, you see. He was there with

his latest little boy-toy, shopping for ladies' lingerie. They were
making that disgusting—what was the name of that thing?
that fairy film—*The Wings*, it was called. And so they ran into
Selma and it was kissy-kissy, hug-hug, of course, a grand re-
union, and you know how charming that old horse-face can be.
And so then Selma said that she was trying on costumes for
Love's Victory and Stiller and his little love-butt were just transported with joy and shrieked that they would help her, and then
everything she had picked out was shoved aside and Maurie
and his little weasel had a grand old time finding the worst-
fitting, most ridiculous and absurd articles they could find for
poor, plump, gullible, grateful Selma. The whole toilette came
to four thousand, eight hundred crowns, almost a fifth of our
budget. You can just imagine, Charlie, how I felt when Selma
came back and modeled that getup. I cried and pleaded, but it
was no use—Selma was as fixed as granite: Stiller was a great
artist, he was, and a true aesthete, he knew his women and in
his generosity he had taken the time to pick out the most beautiful clothes in the world for stupid little Selma. And I should
just shut my mouth and be grateful. That was probably the last
straw for Selma and me. Sure, we had messed around a little
here and there, but we had a damned fine friendship. We cared
for each other, we really did. No, hell, I'm not bitter! (*Laughs*)
But I did get a little lonely. Because Selma left. (*Drinks*) Well,
hell. No, everything was just fine. Everything is fine if you just
make an effort, you know that, my little Caesar! If anyone
does, you do. (*Laughter. Silence. Takes a generous gulp.*) And
then there was that little embarrassment in connection with the
filming of *The Downhill Road*—I had written the script and
was directing, it was late fall and cold as hell—snow in October in southern Sweden, what would be the odds on that? Snow
on the roof of the studio. Well, you know the film was about
morphine—I had tried it a little and there was a nice understanding old doctor who—well. And I had an infected tooth,
too—and then the insomnia—that summer of '16 was ex-

hausting and all of my films had to be edited with my private
life being what it was . . . So there we were in the studio and
Gabriel and Sybil—Smolova—that sweet girl, you know that
was a real woman, Charlie! But she brought her boyfriend
along to the studio all day every day, you couldn't get a piece
of toilet paper between the two of them. So beautiful and
funny. And then Gabriel goes and says something right in the
middle of a take: "bag," he says and stares at me with those fish
eyes, "bag, baaaaag, baaaag." It was so incredibly funny, Gabriel really has a comic genius, so we all started laughing—and
I can't stop laughing, you see—I just keep on laughing and
make a fool of myself out there in the snow outside the studio
and I stand there and laugh until I piss my pants. Then—I
have no idea how the devil it happened—I started to sob and
got dizzy and threw up and lay down in the snow, maybe to
cool down a bit, I'm really on fire, the whole cadaver is just
trembling and boiling, you understand, Charlie. And then
Sybil comes out and puts her arms around me and the others
come out and carry me in and nothing else gets filmed that day.
For the next few days Manne Göthson took over—but then
I'm in good shape again and everything is back to normal—
for the most part. But then after the filming and editing of *The
Downhill Road*, I checked into a sanitarium for a month or so.
The whole time I was there I was working on the scripts for the
next summer, especially *Nocturnal Notes*, which was a great
comfort in my solitude—I didn't want people coming in to
visit me, you see—a lot of people thought I had just gone
completely crazy, you know. But the work on *Nocturnal Notes*
was a comfort and my salvation, you understand. You've seen
it, haven't you, Charlie? Oh, no? Well, that film was probably
my favorite child, or whatever you call it: This guy loves poetry but can't write it himself, and so he steals a real poem from
a true poet and pretends it's his own. He gets his due when he
falls through a trapdoor in the theater and is killed. (*Suddenly,
desperately*) I make my films, Charlie, I do my lighting and

place my camera angles and I tell the actors to walk this way
and do this, and there you're supposed to cry and there you're
in a rage, and we keep on doing it and keep it up like the very
devil and we never give up. And then the audience sits there
one evening, and if we're in luck they'll cry where we decided
they would cry and laugh when we want them to—right. You
know all that. That is the whole mystery, Charlie. Everything
else is shit. There's so much talk nowadays about art and literature and raising the bar and all that noise—you can read the
gentleman's incomprehensible pronouncements in the newspa-
pers. Fine by me—be my guest, Mr. Crybaby Seastrom and
Mr. King of the Queens Stiller, as far as I'm concerned, and be
my guest Emperor Charlie! Raise the bar, sail on the good ship
Art, worship at the altar of Artistry, I tip my hat to you, I lick
your dust, and even so both you and I know that nothing matters but one little point, and that is laughter and tears and the
thing they call "suspense." (*Drinks*) Can you offer an alternative, Emperor of Every Success? Yes, I do go on. And you,
Charlie, stare at me with the eyes of a fried cod—I wonder
how many people you've scared out of their wits with that
stare—or un-stare. You don't scare me, anyway. You know
I'm joking, don't you, old Charlie old pal? You'll let an old
clown pull his Highness's leg a little, right? Right. (*Silence.*)
You just keep mum, and I keep right on talking. It's nice of you
to listen to me. (*Drinks*) Maybe we ought to talk business a little
bit. Not just sit here goofing around. So how's your old Pack-
ard running, Charlie? I heard that you ran over some poor
devil last summer. Maybe it's not such a great idea to drive
when you're half blind? It's a lot safer to keep to the seas,
Charlie. In your magnificent yacht. There you're the king of
the world, right? There you control the raging elements, there
you stand like a real Gothenburg Prospero, Charlie. We'll see
if you put aside your magic wand one day. Or maybe some
fucking Caliban will snatch it out of your hand? Who's Prospero? He's powerful and noble, a fucking nobleman, a magi-

cian, the lead in *The Tempest* by William Shakespeare, you
know who he is, right? All right, come on, let's get down to
business. Since it was actually you who summoned me here—
your letter moved me, Charlie, I can't deny it—especially that
phrase "let us put aside our differences and speak of the
future"—it really sent a ray of sunshine through my heart,
and my wife and I celebrated with a bottle of champagne at
dinner. She wanted me to say hello, by the way, though she
doesn't know you. You must bring your sweet little Emma
Wilhelmina to our house for dinner some evening. Is she as
beautiful as always? Yes, you are a lucky man! Especially considering your looks, Charlie, but "success has balls" as they say
Over There. No, I'm just joking with you, Charlie. You are a
fine, decent person. You are a good man and you deserve every
last ounce of your formidable success. You know that an old
love never rusts and I love you, damn it—you're like a little
brother to me, you know that. So you didn't get mad, did you?
You are and will always be my idol, you know that! (*Laughs*) I
think I could use a little refill. You're not suspicious of me, are
you? Believe it or not, I'm actually a little nervous. You've just
gotten to be so confoundedly big, Charles Magnusson! Who
would have imagined it when we were out there working and
slaving in the Lidingö studio? Do you remember that night, it
must have been in 1912, and that piece of shit Malmberg was
filming—what was the name of that thing again? Oh yeah,
The Judgment of Society—and Velander was drunk and you
and I and Malmberg were putting up the set for the next day's
filming—it was some kind of engagement party with crowds
of extras—damn, Charlie, those were the days! And the lady
who ran the hotel, old lady Roos, came out with coffee and
sandwiches and her pretty daughter and champagne and we
partied until dawn, but we finished that set! Yeah, and so now
it's come to this. (*Pause*) I don't want to waste your precious
time, my dear brother, but I have a serious proposal, which you
ought to consider and which should be (*drinks*) particularly attractive for both Svensk Filmindustri and the Emperor himself.

So now I'll let you in on it. (*He opens his elegant case and takes out a notebook with typewritten pages and a thick volume bound in ox-blood leather.*) So, here comes a project that has been worked out to the last detail, Charlie—and I think—I am convinced that it could be a cinematic sensation. You know how it was. I left Lidingö—they wanted me to be head of the studio, but I couldn't get along with Victor, that stingy, mean, power-hungry, humble little hypocrite. So I took off for Paris and worked with Louis Feuillade, you know, the guy at Fantomas. One day he gave me this book and said, Here's something in your line, Monsieur George, and so he gave me the book. (*Leafs through it*) It is an early edition of a novel called *Justine*, written by a gentleman named Donatien Alphonse de Sade. He lived during the French Revolution and was one hell of a writer. Have you heard of him, Charlie? No, right, of course not. Well, this novel *Justine* is about two sisters, both of them very beautiful and high-class. Juliette is as wild as hell, goes in for every imaginable excess, but Justine, her younger sister, is a paragon of virtue and propriety. Well, the crazy way things turn out, Charlie, it's the *lecherous* sister who lives the high life and makes mountains of money and can afford every possible comfort, while the younger sister, can you imagine, the one who is so damned noble and virtuous and good, is hit with the most beastly adversities until she finally dies as tragically and movingly as anything. (*He shows him the book.*) Look, here's one of the illustrations, this is how a woman like Juliette enter-tains herself on Christmas Eve—pretty sophisticated, huh, Charlie? Turn the book upside down and you can get a better look. That's the life of Riley, wouldn't you say? Four men, right? Five, actually, but he—or is it a she—is hidden by— Now, I don't mean that we should be making smut, Charlie. That's absolutely not my style and besides, it's impossible with our bright-eyed censors. No, this is how I've imagined it: We build a theater set and raise the curtain on the Marquis de Sade with his book, and then he tells the tragic and terrible story of the two sisters. While he speaks, the scenes are played on our little stage. And all the locales are painted on beautiful backgrounds that can be moved at lightning speed. I have actually spoken with Grabow and he promised to give us a good price—we would need thirty-odd scenes and Grabow said that he himself would enjoy the experiment. And then we have the world's best cast, Charlie! Can you see Mary Jonsson as the innocent sister! No one would be better than Mary—she is about to be an international star, Charlie! It's just a question of time before the Americans step in and buy her away from us. She has an inspiring beauty and such moist eyes and she's so little and delicate but so feminine at the same time, you must have seen her in *The Lighthouse Keeper's Daughter*—you didn't? But I can show it to you. And Maja Cassel can play the bad sister. Have you seen her biceps or shoulders, Charlie? And the luster of her skin and her smile? There's a hidden sinfulness there, I can tell you. Secret lust and the rawest shamelessness under that polished surface! I'd put my hand in the flames for Maja Cassel, though I haven't been able to put my hand or anything else in there, either. (*Laughs*) No, she's the faithful type. She keeps on living the modest life with her boring husband. But that's just the kind of girl that's most interesting: fire under the ice! If you know what I mean. (*More eagerly*) And who would be greater than Calle Barcklind as the Marquis? You know how the women are wild for Calle? They'd eat him for breakfast if they could. He glows with tragic manliness. He walks as if he's carrying a heavy load between his legs—and he is—we've been in the sauna together, and I'm telling you! (*Laughs*) Women can sense that kind of thing, God knows how, but Calle brings a special kind of aroma to the box office. Now we're getting to the most important part, Charlie. I can really understand if you don't want to have me messing around in your fine new studio out there in Råsunda—by the way, was there really an ostrich farm on the property before you bought it? Is that really true? Well, I don't know why that's so funny, but there's something inexpressibly sublime about putting a studio on an ostrich farm—oh, of course, I can understand that you don't want me there; I can respect that. And I would just get into it with Victor and Maurie. They want to keep their little fiefdom to themselves—I understand that. But listen, Charlie—the Hasselblad studio in Gothenburg is still there; I've been out there to look it over, and of course it's a little rough around the edges after standing empty and deserted for more than a year, but it would be easy to work it up, Charlie! We could do it in no time flat. And I can get all the technicians I need, good people, too, after all, we did make twenty-seven films in three summers, Charlie. We know our stuff, and Florin—our cameraman, you know—is available, right now he's making ads for Tullberg. He started crying for joy when I asked him if he wanted to do a big project with me again! And the lab won't pose much of a problem, either. Didriksen at Hasselblad says that the old machines haven't been torn down, they're still up and as good as they ever were, and the Lund brothers say they're willing to come back any day, even though they're officially retired. And Hasselblad has nothing against renting out its facilities to Svensk Filmindustri. The equipment is just rotting away out there. Jesus, Charlie! This thing will be fantastic. And I'll turn all the credit over to you if you lend me a hand. (*He hands him a piece of paper with complex tables and figures.*) Here's an estimate of what the whole shebang will cost. Only about twenty-four thousand crowns! And the profits are yours to keep. Hasselblad wants to retain rights to a modest amount for any administrative costs and the maintenance of a studio. I haven't included that figure in my calculations, but I can't imagine that it would amount to much. (*Eager, emotional*) Well, Charlie old boy, now you know why Georgie has been giving you such frightened looks, just like an old dog that's about to be shot. Now you know why the rumor mill has been running like loose bowels: I'm no genius, Charlie. I'm really not. I'm not like those so-called giants Victor and Maurie who've turned your head with their genteel ways and all that loose talk about art this and art that. I'm not a genius, I am a craftsman, Charlie, a damned good and experienced craftsman and I put out a good product, really useful goods that ordinary people need on a regular basis to feel a little better, to help them forget all the bullshit. To let them cry and laugh and maybe scare them a little. I have made twenty-six films, Charlie. I am good at it and I could get even better if I'm just given another chance. I'm only forty years old— forty-two, to be exact. I have loads of plans, ideas, and proposals, Charlie. You don't need to give me a salary, just pay me a little bit per film, enough to keep my head above water. You would never have any trouble with your little company down there in Gothenburg, but we would make films for you, fine, well-made films for you to screen in your all-too-many and far-too-big theaters—you simply won't be able to manage without us! My weakness and weariness are history, I'm ready to get going on something big. You and your boys say: "We shall turn to literature. There's where we'll find what today's people need and want." I say, "Sure! But we don't have to hang on old lady Lagerlöf's apron strings all the time, damn it all!" There are other books in the world. Have you ever read Heidenstam, Charlie? Or Hans Alienus? No, of course, you've had other things on your mind, I can tell that by looking at your elegant office and your elegant secretary and Victor's new car and Maurie's new little love-butt. But that Hans Alienus is a real star, see. He could be the next big thing in all of Europe, in all the world! Hans Alienus, Charlie. *The humane in the human!* The Seeker, the Adventurer. A modern Faust. (*Declaims*)

> I have seen centuries in a second
> I know no hymn with words great enough
> I arrive elated, dazzled, delirious, and hot
> I have played on the meadows with the happy young.
> I have cried myself to sleep with bliss
> Hear the thunder of the dance—hear the song of Hades'
>   daughters!

(*Blows his nose*) Well. Well. Tears always come to my eyes
when I read Hans Alienus' farewell from his deathbed—I
don't know what it is, it reminds me of home somehow, I
guess. Can you imagine the incredible film that would make:
Alienus in Hellas, at the Carnival in Venice, in the Realm of the
Dead. With our friend Gabriel Alw—what do you think?
Here's the book, Charlie, read it and let it move you. After all,
you're a man of great thoughts and broad vistas. You're no ordinary Joe; you're a phenomenon! Don't think I'm flattering
you! Just let me compete this once with your eagles, your
geniuses—just this once. If I fail, you can make an errand boy
out of me. I'll crawl humbly back to my little farces with mean
mothers-in-law, crazy fox terriers, and underwear. That's a
deal. What do you say (*drinks*) to sealing the deal with a classy
dinner, Charlie! Just like the good old days. And we'll bring the
prettiest girls along for company. It'll be fun, Charlie. You
could use some human contact to give you a break from all
your soulful giants and bank directors, and that cold-blooded
lizard Ivar Krueger. How the hell can you team up with that
monster? Before you know it, he'll have gobbled you up, slurp,
burp, and you won't even amount to a sorry sack of shit. Oh,
excuse me, I'm running off at the mouth. Well, my glass is
empty and the bottle is emptier than it ought to be. And here I
stand on your genuine Persian rug and see that you have a little
Elias Martin hanging on the wall, no, damn, it's a John Fredrik
Martin, they're a little hard to tell apart—here I stand, Charles
Magnusson, and offer you my talent, my industry, my intelli-
gence, and my passion. If "passion" seems a little dramatic, let
us say "horniness." I will be your capable servant, your courageous samurai, your most loyal dog. Take me, use me, test
me—it will cost you a trifle and you'll get it back more than
sevenfold. I'm begging you, Charlie. I'm going down on my
knees (*kneels*), maybe it seems a little artificial, but it's a true
expression of my despair and my hope. Brother Charlie, be as
wise as people say you are. Be as generous as the rumors say.

Be as kindhearted as I know you are and give me your hand and bring me back to life. You are the only one who can help me, all the others are gone, dead, devoured. You have crushed everyone in your path, you are the victor, you are the only one who can give me back my life, yes, I know I said that already, but it's worth repeating. I'm on my knees before you, Charles Magnusson, and I can see your little head sticking up over that gigantic black desk and you are looking at me through the lenses of your glasses. I can't see your eyes, maybe you're not looking at me at all, you are so damned walleyed, maybe you're looking at the clock, yes, of course I know, I have kept you long enough, I've had my say. (*Gets up*) Now you know, Charlie, you know where you have me. And now you know that the life I've been living ever since *The Lighthouse Keeper's Daughter* has not been a life worth living. I have disgraced myself beyond the bounds of what is proper and I am quite satisfied with having disgraced myself. Did you know that I have three brothers who are all big guns in Swedish society? A professor, a judge, and a general. When they catch sight of me, they cross the street. (*Sits down, takes a swig from the bottle*) Empty and drinking myself to death, my dear friend, I can hear the death-watch ticking. Do you remember Emma, by the by? No, of course not, you're one of those practical types who forget embarrassments. Emma, Charlie? Emma Andersson? Out at Lidingö, she was the one always helping, helping, and was everywhere at once and was so kind and so big and clumsy and happy? She was cute, too, with her potato nose and her stylish little breasts and an ass that— You don't remember Emma? Well, brother Charlie. Since I was the head of the studio I had certain—no, it's not what you're thinking—she wasn't my type, there were others who—well, there was no need for a guy to sleep alone in those days if he was afraid of the dark, I mean. (*Grins*) Well, Emma used to talk about her "submarine." Nobody knew what she meant and she always laughed when she talked about that "submarine." Then she moved with us

down to Hasselblad in Gothenburg and she was a little worse
for wear by then, but still happy. And clever and helpful, she
started a thing with our friend Jonny—Jonny Ekman, you
know, the one who painted watercolors—and he painted her
both clothed and in the buff. Well, one day I asked her how her
"submarine" was doing. If she still had it and whether she was
thinking about taking it out on the west coast. Then she
laughed and said that she was going to take it for a spin on Sat-
urday, all by herself. And that's what Emma did. She rented a
rowboat out at Särö, it was a beautiful, cool, autumn day and
the sea was so still with just a little swell. Emma rowed out a bit
and looked into the sun, sat there for a long time and looked
into the sun and blinded herself. Then she chained herself to
the boat, threw the oars overboard, and pulled out the cork.
And she sank out there with the sun into the darkening water.
That was Emma's "submarine." (*Drinks*) About that thing with
Justine and Juliette. You don't need to give your answer right
away, of course you'll have to think it over, Charlie. I can understand that. Twenty-four thousand crowns is twenty-four
thousand crowns, after all, and I know you have four bankers
on the board and your buddy Ivar Krueger, for Christ's sake.
So there's not quite as much independence as there once was,
am I right? Now I'm going to take a sniff at your liquor cabinet
and see if there is any cure in there for a thirsty devil. (*He grubs
around loudly in the cabinet. Clinks and clanks. Suddenly locates a
bottle of cognac.*) Do you remember the Powderhouse out at
Lidingö? Four departments. One for the staff, one for the artists, one for the administration, and one for Victor and his hem-
orrhoids. What a great cognac! I didn't think that you—
excuse me? Here's to the Powderhouse at Lidingö and while
we're at it, here's to Selma's sweet rosy-red ass— "The heights
of lustification," if one may say so! (*Drinks out of the bottle*) No.
Now I'm going. You can keep the book about the two sisters. I
assume that your French is, shall we say, a little rusty—but
you can always look at the pictures with your Emma Wil-

helmina. And here is my draft of the script, by the way, neatly written in thirty-eight scenes, and so maybe I'll hear from you some day—I'll be waiting by the phone. The number is at the bottom of the last page. I'll just pray that the telephone won't be disconnected. It's been a little dicey on that front these last few weeks. And so farewell, my brother; God be with you. I am worried about your future, I want you to know. If you weren't so charmingly ignorant I would refer you to Greek tragedy, where the gods pour their wrath on human beings who think that they're gods. It's called hubris, in case you haven't heard. (*He kisses* MAGNUSSON *on the forehead.*) And so farewell—we will never meet again—I know that. You have flushed me down the filmmaking toilet forever. In your eyes I'm just a shabby little ghost from the past—isn't that so, my former brother? (*He removes* CHARLES MAGNUSSON's *glasses.*) Aha! So that's how you look these days, my poor little traitor! You know, I feel sorry for you, you have nothing left. You have sold your soul to Power and his archangels, the bankers and that terrifying Yahweh called Ivar Krueger. Believe me, believe me, in five years you'll be out on the street, my poor Charlie. Look at me, look at me. You must believe I'm mad. You're thinking and thinking, the thoughts are just whirring around in that well-combed little head: he's lost his mind, that Klercker, I'd better not move a muscle. (*He returns* MAGNUSSON's *glasses tenderly.*) So you keep your distance, keep your distance, keep your distance, even when you're humping. Our mutual friend Adela can testify to that—you must remember Adela? She said that you had come up with a humping technique where nothing but your genitals were supposed to touch. And when the thing was over and done with you would rush out to the bathroom and wash and wash and wash, because of your germ phobia. You poor little wimp, growing flowers you don't even know the names of and your pitiful piano playing and all your book-shelves lined with unread books. And that sailboat of yours that you always run aground. What was the role you wanted to

play, exactly, you tweedy little upstart? Can you tell me that? I
read in some paper that you claim your father was an "archi-
tect." What a story, Charlie! Your father was a shitty little
draughtsman of the lowest order whose name happened to be
Salomon Magnusson, a half-Jew, and you lived on the poor
side of town in two little rooms! Embarrassing, huh? What a
lowlife you are, Magnusson. Not because you were poor, but
for the simple reason that you deny your own origins. That's
low, Magnusson, that's as low as you can go. But you'll get
yours, because when the bad times come—and they will come,
you can be sure of that—when the bad times come you'll simply blow away, because then you will be no one at all! (*He
walks to the door, turns around, and aims a pistol at* MAGNUSSON.)
Yes, Charles Magnusson, it is really true! Totally real! This is
Death looking you in the eye through this little machine,
equipped with two bullets, one for you and one for me. This is
no contemptible melodrama made in the Hasselblad studio nor
a brilliant piece thrown together by Svensk Filmindustri, but a
well-conceived scene taken straight from life's brutality, a lyri-
cal and thought-provoking scene, Charles Magnusson. You
have taken my life, and now I will take yours. I promise that
there won't be any stains on your expensive rug or the elegant
painting by Bonnard, maybe just a little brain matter on the
wallpaper behind you and a splash of the same substance on the
bookshelf. Everything will happen quickly and painlessly, I assure you. During my military service I was a gold medalist in
marksmanship—well, that's about it, Mr. Magnusson. Putting
your hands up will really do no good at all, try to be calm and
dignified instead—after all, you have created great work in
your life. And you can be grateful for that. You should also be
grateful to me for ending your life while it's at its apex. Because
it's all downhill from here, straight downhill into catastrophe.
Farewell, Charlie, we probably won't be seeing each other
over there in the realm of shades or on the ferry over the Styx.
You'll probably be traveling first class, as always. Don't

tremble so, Mr. Magnusson—and— No, don't try to hide under the desk. I can't deny that this is one of the most satisfying moments in my poor lost life, even if it has to be the last.

GEORG AF KLERCKER fires the pistol. A cigarette falls out of the barrel and a little flame shoots out. He lights the cigarette and puts the pistol into his pocket. He begins to laugh. The laughter turns into sobs. He falls down on his hands and knees and pounds his head against the floor.

I beg of you, Charlie, please. Good God, Charlie, have a little *mercy*—we used to be friends, after all—have mercy, I beg of you.

Silence.

CHARLES MAGNUSSON (*speaks into the intercom*) Would you be kind enough to ask security to come up immediately, Miss Holm?

GEORG AF KLERCKER No, no. (*Calms himself*) Not that humiliation. I'll be all right. Don't worry Magnusson. Don't worry. I'll leave on my own.

GEORG AF KLERCKER arranges his clothes, smoothes his hair, and blows his nose. He stands at attention. After a few seconds, he gives MAGNUSSON a winning, childish smile. MAGNUSSON rises and walks toward AF KLERCKER with his hand extended. The lieutenant turns abruptly away and walks out the door, which he closes carefully. MAGNUSSON stands there, a bit nonplussed—perhaps a bit hurt—with his outstreched hand and an empty smile on his thin, gray lips. Then he takes a deep breath and walks energetically to his gleaming black desk. Once again he picks up the intercom receiver.

CHARLES MAGNUSSON Hello, Miss Holm! No, no, security won't be necessary. Yes, I understand, the guard had gone to lunch. Another thing, Miss Holm! Who is the head of the committee for free tickets? I can't recall . . . Oh, yes, our friend Hedberg. Certainly. Right. Would you be so kind as to call

Hedberg and tell him from me that Lieutenant af Klercker's free pass to Swedish cinemas should be canceled as of the first of January. He can say "for just cause." That will suffice. Thank you. Yes, I am going to lunch now and will back after two. Good afternoon, Miss Holm.

MAGNUSSON hangs up. He exits the room.

IN THE PRESENCE
OF A CLOWN

There is on the outer periphery of the family chronicle a brief announcement in few words telling of the engagement between Carl Åkerblom, engineer, and Pauline Thibault, a gym instructress. At the time, he was fifty-four and she was twenty-two.

I have a fragmentary memory of a visit by the contracting parties to my grandmother's house in Trädgårdsgatan in Uppsala. I knew Uncle Carl well. He was my favorite, and the fact that he had what in those days (1925) was called "weak nerves" was unimportant. He was playful, inventive, and treated me as a contemporary. He also had an almost unlimited repertoire of conjuring tricks. My memory of Miss Thibault is blurred, like a photograph in which the subject has moved in mid-exposure. She was tall, broad-shouldered, thin, dark-haired, well-groomed, pale, and dark-eyed. I think she had burning eyes, but that may well be subsequent rationalization. When she smiled, she revealed a row of dazzlingly white teeth, but that

---

Translator's notes may be found on page 153.

may also be imagination. On a later occasion, one evening when the newly betrothed couple had had dinner with the family, she played the piano and sang with a dark, resonant musicality. I was not present, as the concert was after my bedtime, but I remember the stillness of that winter evening, a jangling sledge down in the street, the humming in the tiled stove, and then that dark voice. It was all sorrowful, but indescribably pleasant. There, my memory of Pauline Thibault comes to an end. Later research shows that their engagement was broken off after a few years and Uncle Carl returned to hospital. Miss Thibault vanished to Germany, probably Berlin.

Yet another circumstance: In the brief inventory of Uncle Carl's belongings, what was called a sciopticon was noted, equipped with an arc lamp, reflecting mirror, and Zeiss lens. The machine was kept in a brown-stained oak box with brass handles on the lid and at the ends. Two hundred glass slides, eleven by eleven centimeters (hand-colored), were kept upright in four well-preserved wooden boxes, fifty slides in each, as well as detailed descriptions of the contents on the inside of the lid. As far as I can remember, those in the series were called: *Walks with Jesus*, *The River Dal from Source to Sea*, *The Human Body*, and, finally, *Schumann and Beethoven: Their Times and Music*. In the description of the last of these, there were references to appropriate pieces of music, transposed for piano. They have been supplemented, with neatly written instructions in red ink, presumably done by Pauline Thibault.

That's how they look, our sources.

Carl Åkerblom and Pauline Thibault are traveling through icy winter country: he is to give lectures and show hand-colored slides and she is to play and sing.

Like that, more or less—though slightly different.

Characters

CARL ÅKERBLOM Engineer and inventor, 54

PAULINE THIBAULT Gymnastics instructress, Carl's fiancée, 22

ANNA ÅKERBLOM Carl's stepmother. Widow, 66

KARIN BERGMAN Carl's half sister, 34

OSVALD VOGLER Professor Emeritus, 75

EMMA VOGLER His wife. Deaf-mute, 48

JOHAN EGERMAN Doctor, 40

NURSE STELLA Ward nurse, 50

MIA FALK Actress, 20

RIGMOR THE CLOWN Ageless

PETRUS LANDAHL Carpentry teacher, 32

ALMA BERGLUND Farmer, 60

MÄRTA LUNDBERG Teacher, 42

KARIN PERSSON Widow, 46

ALGOD FRÖVIK Sexton, 58

STEFAN LARSSON Chief superintendent, 58

HANNA APELBLAD Bakery owner, 47

FREDRIK BLOM Organist, in early retirement, 56

TWO POLICEMEN

TWO ASSISTANT NURSES

TITLE
Life's but a walking shadow . . .

TITLE
. . . A poor player,
That struts and frets his hour upon the stage,
And then is heard no more.

TITLE
It is a tale
Told by an idiot . . .

TITLE
. . . Signifying nothing.
—Shakespeare's *Macbeth*

ACT I

Scene 1

It is the end of October 1925, and at the moment the scene is a ward in the Uppsala University Hospital Psychiatric Department. The ward contains six beds, three along each long wall. Two high-barred windows face an angled brick facade of prison-like appearance. A leafless tree is just visible. Between the windows, a heavy wooden table is bolted to the floor, and around the table six sturdy wooden chairs stand guard.

MAIN TITLE

IN THE PRESENCE OF A CLOWN

TITLE

Uppsala Asylum
October
1925

Until further notice, only one patient is to be in this ward. His name is CARL ÅKERBLOM, an engineer by profession and fifty-four years old, heavy-shouldered, a child's rosy complexion, slightly chubby.

His hair is thick and graying, thinning on top, a well-groomed beard. A cigar stump between his bluish-white lips. On his bed is the local paper, Upsala Nya Tidning. *He is in night attire, seated on the foot of the bed. In front of him, on a bedside table, is a gramophone; he puts the needle down on a record and music emerges: it is Schubert's "Der Leiermann." He lets it play for a second or two and then lifts the needle, putting it down again at the beginning of the record, starting the music again. He repeats this action a couple of times.*

In the corridor JOHAN EGERMAN *and* NURSE *can be heard talking. The door is suddenly unlocked and in comes* DOCTOR EGERMAN, *tall, white-coated, his hair trim and his beard and mustache dark and glossy.* ÅKERBLOM *swiftly removes the gramophone and puts a jug and wash basin on the table instead.*

EGERMAN How is the patient, eh?

NURSE Well, the patient has been somewhat restless and depressed, so I put him in a ward where he could be on his own a little.

EGERMAN Let us have a look in any case.

EGERMAN and NURSE *go in.*

EGERMAN Good evening, Mr. Åkerblom.

ÅKERBLOM lies down on the bed and starts reading the paper.

EGERMAN You may wait outside, Nurse.

NURSE Of course, Dr. Egerman.

NURSE leaves at suitable speed.

EGERMAN Good evening, Mr. Åkerblom.

ÅKERBLOM Good evening, Doctor.

EGERMAN Might I perhaps ask you a few questions?

ÅKERBLOM Of course, Dr. Egerman.

EGERMAN sits on a chair at the foot of the bed.

ÅKERBLOM Provided I may ask one first . . .

EGERMAN But of course.

ÅKERBLOM . . . if you have the time.

EGERMAN Limited.

ÅKERBLOM rapidly moves closer to Egerman.

ÅKERBLOM What do you think Franz Schubert felt like, that Tuesday morning in April, 1823? It had snowed the previous night and the tiled stove had gone out.

EGERMAN Um, what he felt like?

ÅKERBLOM What did he feel? He's sitting on his bed in his nightshirt, warmed by a large cardigan, woolen socks on his feet. He has his chamber pot between his knees and is just going to urinate. As this business causes him a little pain, he has pulled back his foreskin and widened the actual opening. Then he spots the sore. It is just below the edge of the glans, a sore and a taut hardening where there had previously been nothing but a dark redness—ugly, yet not tender. At that moment, at six in the morning exactly, the bells tinkle in nearby Trinity Church. At that instant, Franz Schubert realizes he has syphilis; and now I want to know what you think his feelings are, Dr. Egerman, that April morning as he sits on his bed looking at his sick willie.

EGERMAN Well now, Mr. Åkerblom, that's not very easy to guess.

ÅKERBLOM The evening before, he'd been to supper at his brother Ferdinand's house. The party was bright and cheerful. Beautiful, talented ladies, witty, charming gentlemen. They have played games, made music, and sung. Happiness, dancing, music. Then home that night through the still damp snow. Happiness—no drunkenness. But then . . . syphilis. What do you think Franz Schubert is feeling, Dr. Egerman, as he sits there?

EGERMAN I think he has the sensation of a kind of sinking.

ÅKERBLOM Sinking?

EGERMAN A sinking feeling.

ÅKERBLOM Why, Doctor, do you think he has a sinking feeling?

EGERMAN I was thinking about how I myself—a sinking into horror. Suffocation. Enclosed.

ÅKERBLOM No notes of music to help him.

EGERMAN No notes, no.

ÅKERBLOM Yes. Yes. Horror of horrors. You wanted to ask some questions, Dr. Egerman.

ÅKERBLOM makes himself comfortable in the bed again. EGERMAN stands up, reads the casebook, and sits on another chair, a little farther away.

EGERMAN Yes, yes, of course. Mr. Åkerblom, do you yourself consider you are ill, with "weak nerves" as your casebook has it? Moreover: mania, visions, outbursts, muddled thoughts, state of confusion, depression, inexplicable euphoria, self-recrimination, sexual fantasies, suicidal conjecture, overestimation of self, hypochondria, infantile fecal activities, but most of all, of course, *violence.*

ÅKERBLOM laughs. Then, after a pause:

ÅKERBLOM Was that all?

EGERMAN Yes, well, I suppose that is all. Mr. Åkerblom, you once said that your real profession was that of "the inventor's vocation and vision"?

ÅKERBLOM Exactly. For twenty-nine years I have besieged the Royal Patent Office with applications, but only twice have they, in their mercy, granted me a patent.

EGERMAN Your fiancée, Pauline Thibault, wishes to visit you.

ÅKERBLOM No, no, no!

EGERMAN She says you have forbidden her to come.

ÅKERBLOM No, no . . .

EGERMAN Are we not to mention Miss Thibault?

ÅKERBLOM Preferably *not*.

EGERMAN Dare I ask why?

ÅKERBLOM Because it *pains* me, dear Doctor!

EGERMAN makes a note in the casebook.

EGERMAN So, she can't visit?

ÅKERBLOM Dr. Egerman, the moment you came in just now, you pointed out that you were in a hurry. I have no desire to keep you.

EGERMAN Right! Until we meet again, Mr. Åkerblom.

ÅKERBLOM Dr. Egerman . . . I liked what you thought about Schubert. I mean that "sinking."

EGERMAN I'm glad to hear it. Goodnight.

ÅKERBLOM Goodnight, Doctor.

DR. EGERMAN hurries out. A nursing assistant and an elderly gentleman approach rapidly down the corridor. The door is un-locked and a fat ASSISTANT NURSE appears. She ushers in an eld-erly, gangling gentleman, extremely well-dressed, his eyes bright behind the thick lenses of his glasses. He at once sees Mr. Åkerblom and hurries over, with outstretched hand.

VOGLER Osvald Vogler "at your service," as we used to say in the old days.

ÅKERBLOM Åkerblom.

VOGLER Osvald Vogler's the name, retired professor in exegesis at the city's university, and—and I'm not ashamed to mention it—of independent means.

VOGLER addresses the ASSISTANT.

VOGLER Thank you, my dove. Would you please put my case by my bed and I'll manage the unpacking myself. Here! A little something for you trouble.

The ASSISTANT retreats and locks the door. VOGLER looks at his pocket watch, gets a little book out, and makes a note.

VOGLER Well . . . Arrived at asylum at thirteen minutes past five.

ÅKERBLOM Excuse me.

VOGLER By all means.

ÅKERBLOM I'm sicker than I look.

VOGLER Yes, our freedom is restricted, I must admit, and freedom is God's gift to the children of man. But don't let's be niggardly, and instead compare the importance of outer freedom as such, so to speak, with inner freedom, the subjective, by Self uninterruptedly conceived and by Self unfortunately also uninterruptedly destroying freedom, what we *call* "inner freedom"; as it consists of such a large number of components, which are impossible to codify, analyze, or classify. And, and . . . Let's sit down . . . Since freedom is the most elevated characteristic of the human spirit, the ancient source of the Sacred One and the sole and literal immortality of Life. Our incarceration in this humiliating prison of the body is thus a nullity which is not to disturb the flight of our thoughts. Inner freedom is what we understand of what has previously been said, however threatened it may seem to be, an enrapturing incontrovertible fact which we hold in our carefully cupped hands as we raise them to the eternal light. At the same time, for your information, I should mention I am a member of a worldwide society. Its name is "L'Esclavage rompu, ou la Société des Péteurs du Monde." Liberté est notre devise.

After some silence.

ÅKERBLOM And what are the aims and the point of your society, if I may be so bold?

VOGLER Our society eagerly supports free farting. We combat the European slavery of farting.

ÅKERBLOM I don't like to boast, but I can actually extinguish four lighted candles with one single but powerful fart.

VOGLER laughs and pats ÅKERBLOM on the cheek.

VOGLER We must be allowed to fantasize, in our appalling situation. I'm not just talking about you and me, but about Humanity, the situation as a whole, seen from the perspective of the enlightened human spirit; we must invest in joint enterprises, Mr. Åkerblom; and in that way combat chaos and decay! Now . . . here . . . at this very moment . . .

ÅKERBLOM (*in a faint whisper*) Yes?

VOGLER falls silent.

VOGLER What was I going to say?

ÅKERBLOM Joint enterprises?

VOGLER "Joint enterprises"? Ah, yes . . . That's the way of the world . . .

Silence. VOGLER hides his face in his hands.

VOGLER My dear Mr. Åkerblom! What kind of ill-health forces you to dwell in these singularly depressing premises?

ÅKERBLOM Murderous rage.

VOGLER I beg your pardon?

ÅKERBLOM I almost took someone's life. Killed someone.

ÅKERBLOM gestures, demonstrating a rapid blow.

VOGLER Indeed!

ÅKERBLOM I was afflicted with cramp in my jaw muscles and ground six molars to pieces.

ÅKERBLOM pulls his mouth back with a finger to let Vogler see.

ÅKERBLOM The person who tried to help me out of this terrifying—how shall I put it—difficulty, was rewarded with a murderous blow from a chair leg so that the skin of the forehead split and blood spurted. Luckily the skull was not broken; it amounted only to an insignificant fracture.

VOGLER Highly interesting, I must say.

ÅKERBLOM No, no. I am not interesting in the slightest. Schubert is interesting, on the other hand.

Scene 2

ÅKERBLOM stretches out on his bed. VOGLER sits, feet up, on the bed opposite, and reads a slim book in which he is becoming engrossed.

Silence.

ÅKERBLOM Excuse me for asking, but what are you reading, Professor Vogler?

VOGLER It's *The Confessions of Countess Mizzi*, Vienna, 1909.

ÅKERBLOM's eyes are now closed.

ÅKERBLOM Oh, do tell me!

VOGLER The girl's name was Mizzi Veith, you see, and she was born in one of Vienna's suburbs in 1884. Between 1904 and 1908, she was the most sought after, how shall I put it, "object of desire" in the city.

ÅKERBLOM I say, I say!

VOGLER Mizzi's mother married a certain Herr Marcell Veith and the child was made legitimate. Herr Veith had no profession, but made out he was a Roman count. At fourteen, then, the little "countess" enters the city's gallant circles on her stepfather's hand. As I perhaps forgot to point out . . .

VOGLER holds the book up for ÅKERBLOM to see.

VOGLER . . . the girl was sensationally lovely, a Viennese suburban beauty. Within a year she was hugely talked about and it was said that she did everything except one particular thing. What this was, was never mentioned. In the late autumn of 1908, she took her young life. She left behind a little diary which the father sold to an unscrupulous publisher. At Mizzi's postmortem, it was found that she was still a virgin. Are you asleep, Mr. Åkerblom?

ÅKERBLOM Yes, but I can hear very well all the same.

VOGLER "I am asleep, but I'm listening." Excellent! Did I mention that my wife is a deaf-mute? She is also rich and I live well on her wealth. Mr. Åkerblom? Hallo there! Swedenborg occasionally comes to me in visions, and tells me about the inconceivable beauty of the angels. They reflect the features of God, and Swedenborg looks at me with his smiling, pale gray eyes and says: "Believe you me, Professor Vogler, *I have seen them.*" And then I find the courage to make my way into mysterious worlds, worlds beyond other worlds, and my universe reflects eternity. And as I travel, the insight grows that I, Osvald Vogler, will at any moment be allowed to see The Eternal One as if in a mirrror.[1]

ÅKERBLOM looks up.

ÅKERBLOM And what does he look like?

VOGLER This is what Swedenborg says: "We read that man was created in God's image and in His own likeness." What is meant here by God's image is *divine wisdom* and by likeness is meant *divine love.*

ÅKERBLOM Yes, yes, yes, but what does he look like?

VOGLER He is my image, or I his.

ÅKERBLOM speaks cautiously.

ÅKERBLOM Could it possibly be, Professor, that you are God?

VOGLER It wouldn't surprise me.

EMMA VOGLER comes running down the corridor, loudly wailing. The door is flung open and she enters at high speed. She is a stately lady, forty-eight, elegant and in tears.

ASSISTANT NURSE Calm, please!

With an unarticulated cry, EMMA VOGLER embraces her husband and kisses him anywhere she can get access. TWO ASSISTANTS also tumble in, but stop in timid dismay. Last to enter is DR. EGERMAN. He looks as though he has been floored in the rush.

VOGLER Mr. Åkerblom, my wife—Mrs. Vogler.

EMMA VOGLER takes CARL ÅKERBLOM's hand and shakes it vigorously.

ÅKERBLOM A pleasure.

EMMA VOGLER turns to DR. EGERMAN and starts using sign language.

VOGLER Emma, wait a moment! This is what my wife says: "My husband . . . is my life. I refuse, refuse . . . to let my love be kept in an asylum! He maintains he is a drag on me. Not true. In the letter Dr. Egerman has in his left hand, I have begged the doctor to let my husband go."

EGERMAN True. You are released until further notice.

VOGLER Goodbye and hope to see you again soon, Mr. Åkerblom.

VOGLER embraces ÅKERBLOM and hurries over to the door, pulled by his WIFE.

VOGLER Thank you . . . thank you . . . thank you, Doctor.

DR. EGERMAN slumps onto a bed.

EGERMAN God, how tired I am!

DR. EGERMAN gets up from the bed and shakes ÅKERBLOM's hand.

EGERMAN Goodbye, Mr. Åkerblom.

EGERMAN moves towards the door.

EGERMAN I am so tired.

The ASSISTANT NURSE closes the door behind him as she and EGERMAN leave.

Scene 3

Dusk. The street lighting comes on, casting shadows across the ceiling. ÅKERBLOM is seated on his bed. On the floor, at his feet, is the gramophone, which he starts up. It's is the same piece as earlier.

He manages to hear a couple of bars before the door is unlocked and
NURSE STELLA enters, carrying a small tray with a glass of water
and packets of powders. She switches on the ceiling lights—a dour
and grubby yellow glow.

NURSE STELLA That's right, jump into bed . . . beddy-byes
now!

ÅKERBLOM "Beddy-byes." That sounds nice.

NURSE STELLA Now we'll take our powders, and then
everything'll be much easier . . .

ÅKERBLOM What? No, not the powder.

NURSE STELLA . . . and we'll sleep as soundly as in mother's
arms.

ÅKERBLOM No, not the powder! No!

NURSE STELLA I'll let you off tonight, then. But don't let Dr.
Egerman know.

ÅKERBLOM Christ, no! Don't go, Nurse Stella. Dear Nurse
Stella, my evening star. Sit here on the edge of the bed and
I'll tell you how it is. For the sake of the mercy of God, Nurse
Stella. I'll tell you everything and it'll be over in a couple
of minutes. In the old days they used to punish criminals by
inserting a sharp wooden stake into the arse of the delin-
quent . . .

NURSE STELLA How frightful . . .

ÅKERBLOM . . .Yes, yes . . .Then, with light blows of a
mallet, drive it up through the victim's body so the tip eventually emerged again at the nape of the neck. Then they raised
the stake down by the river, and there the wretch hung. That's
how it is, Nurse Stella. I lived skewered on a stake, and people
pass, down by the bridge; and I am a sight worth seeing . . .
Don't go, Nurse Stella, don't go . . . Don't think I'm asking
for pity, like Jesus or Mahler, or August S.,[2] sentimental old
whiner! No, Schubert, Nurse Stella, Schubert, Franz, is my

friend, my beloved brother. Well, that's all. You do understand, Nurse Stella, don't you?

NURSE STELLA No. You can't ask that of me.

NURSE STELLA tucks him in.

NURSE STELLA Sleep tight, now. Sleep tight and say your evening prayers, if you have any.

ÅKERBLOM I can say them backwards. Amen happiness given is, loves God whom he, goes happiness, comes happiness, happiness my is hand God's in.

ÅKERBLOM "farts" with his lips.

NURSE STELLA That was rather silly. I don't even want to hear it. Goodnight.

ÅKERBLOM Goodnight.

NURSE STELLA switches off the light and exits, locking the door.

ÅKERBLOM What theater! What an audience!

ÅKERBLOM lies on his side and puts his thumb in his mouth. Death is sitting at a table by the window, playing with its fingers in front of a little red apple. The figure is wearing a silky white, yet grimy, clown costume, its makeup white, mouth black. ÅKERBLOM wakes up.

ÅKERBLOM Have you been here long?

CLOWN Quite a while. Quite . . . a while.

ÅKERBLOM Am I not quite awake?

CLOWN Nope! Yoicks!

The CLOWN skip-steps along the ward to a table; on it an enamel jug and washing bowl, which the CLOWN knocks onto the floor, before perching cross-legged on the tabletop.

CLOWN How are you?

ÅKERBLOM I'm bored. And how are you, Mr. . . . Mr. . . . Mr. Törneman?[3]

CLOWN Törneman was my cousin, who died.

ÅKERBLOM Whatever the case, he was a clever clown who scared me to death when I was a child. I remember it perfectly clearly.

CLOWN For that matter, I'm no mister . . .

Ripping the upper costume open, the CLOWN *reveals a woman's breasts.*

CLOWN . . . if that's of any interest.

ÅKERBLOM So, I'm talking to Your Majesty?

CLOWN Yes.

ÅKERBLOM Well, I'll be . . . well, now . . . And now the time has come?

CLOWN Nope.

ÅKERBLOM I'm always claiming "I'm not afraid." Why should I be afraid? Seeing there's no life after death; because there isn't, is there?

CLOWN I don't strut about with secrets, as 'twere. Is that clear?

ÅKERBLOM Yes, oh yes, quite clear. But one is alone? At the actual moment?

CLOWN Alone. Inevitably.

ÅKERBLOM Or rather—one is always alone. But on occasion the aloneness becomes evident.

CLOWN You are fond of big steam engines, are you not?

ÅKERBLOM Yes?

CLOWN The commanding weight, the ground shaking, the deafening roar . . . and the plume, the plume of suffocating smoke, the hot steam from the pistons and the irresistible speeding wind which both sucks and pushes back . . . By the way, I'm not revealing anything unknown, am I?

ÅKERBLOM No, no.

CLOWN If you think about it, you have always known.

ÅKERBLOM I like to think so.

CLOWN I'm attractive, eh?

ÅKERBLOM Of course! I'm as erect as hell!

CLOWN Have me in my arse!

The CLOWN rips a piece of costume off from the bottom area, leans forward, holding the washstand, and sticking out a bared rump.

CLOWN But do it quickly! No, no, no! Don't touch my breasts! Can you feel me squeezing? Isn't it nice?

ÅKERBLOM No, it's not even nice. Yes, it is!

CLOWN Pinch hold with your nails . . . dig your nails in!

ÅKERBLOM I've got no nails—I bite them!

CLOWN Get your hand off! Stick your thumb up my arse!

The CLOWN and ÅKERBLOM tumble onto the floor, and the washstand falls, breaking.

The CLOWN and ÅKERBLOM are lying together in bed.

ÅKERBLOM Rigmor![4]

The CLOWN smiles a black smile.

CLOWN Yes! Rig . . . Mor. That's my name—Rig . . . Mor.

ÅKERBLOM When I was a child, toward morning, just like this, Your Majesty would dance.

CLOWN Like this?

The CLOWN dances her fingers a step or two on ÅKERBLOM's cheek.

ÅKERBLOM In those days, I was king, too.

CLOWN And now, monsieur Åkerblom?

ÅKERBLOM I don't know . . .

ÅKERBLOM miserably:

. . . don't know.

CLOWN Other rules apply now?

ÅKERBLOM If there were only rules!

CLOWN Non–rules?

ÅKERBLOM It smells mostly like demons. But I suppose demons can be tormented.

Death does not answer. Rigmor the CLOWN's *sharp index fingernail makes an incision between her breasts, leaving a trail of blood. Death vanishes—the blood trail remains.* ÅKERBLOM, *lying in bed, suddenly twists in anguish and presses the electric bell button by the bedhead.*

ÅKERBLOM God, don't let me shit in my pants!

NURSE STELLA unlocks the door, snatches up Åkerblom's worn dressing gown, and wraps it around him.

NURSE STELLA Just calm yourself. We'll be in time; we always are. There you are.

ÅKERBLOM The evil spirits of Hell are tearing at my guts. All the nasty things I've committed against Pauline!

NURSE STELLA She's already here.

Silence reigns for a moment.

ÅKERBLOM What!

NURSE STELLA Miss Thibault is waiting out there, in the office.

ÅKERBLOM Oh God in Heaven! No, no, no . . . Malicious devils!

NURSE STELLA Calm! Calm yourself, now! There.

ÅKERBLOM *suddenly becomes silent, and looks up.*

ÅKERBLOM It's too late.

NURSE STELLA Then we'll clean up that calamity as well.

NURSE STELLA hastily bustles ÅKERBLOM out, a pillow pressed against his backside. PAULINE *steps into the proceedings, stopping for a moment or two at the door and at the barred windows. It has*

started to snow, quietly and beautifully. She lights a cigarette, puts
her hat on the table, and stands, looking out of one of the barred
windows. Her head, now bared, reveals a bandaged forehead.
Pauline is an exquisite beauty of about twenty, tall and fairly slim,
straight shoulders, narrow waist, splendid breasts above the iron
ring of her corset. Her dress leaves her neck bare—encompassed by
a shortish gold chain. Her hair is pulled back and is thin and child-
ish. Her eyes are dark blue, her lips slim and well-sculpted. Her left
hand is weighed down by a broad engagement ring—no other jew-
ellery.

NURSE STELLA pushes ÅKERBLOM—after his express discharge,
now newly washed and still in a cold sweat—through the door,
which she then locks. Bewildered, ÅKERBLOM stands there.

PAULINE You can't escape me. As you see.

ÅKERBLOM Oh, God, your wound!

PAULINE Don't namby-pamby, Åkerblom. It's all stitched and
disinfected.

ÅKERBLOM Will there be a scar?

PAULINE Yes, I expect so.

ÅKERBLOM lies down on the bed.

ÅKERBLOM It was your fault.

PAULINE I haven't come here to haggle over trivialities. You
went mad and struck out. What's to be said of that?

ÅKERBLOM You asked for it.

PAULINE And you asked for the truth.

ÅKERBLOM And now you've come here to reap my contrition
and my begging for forgiveness. But I have to tell you,
Pauline, you'll get none of it.

PAULINE Surely you don't think I've gone as mad as you—
darling?

ÅKERBLOM Then I don't know what you've come for, except possibly to celebrate a cheap triumph at the sight of your future husband's total humiliation.

PAULINE I certainly didn't come here to see your humiliation, my dear Carl Åkerblom. That's been a daily bitter diet all through our engagement.

ÅKERBLOM It didn't sound like that then.

PAULINE I imagined I had a task and that you realized I wanted to help you.

ÅKERBLOM Here comes the bit about my stepmother and her jealousy.

PAULINE You don't even know what you're talking about now.

ÅKERBLOM Ha-ha!

PAULINE What? Me jealous of your stepmother!

ÅKERBLOM I never said so.

PAULINE I don't care what you did say or didn't say. I've got a suggestion.

ÅKERBLOM A suggestion? What kind of suggestion?

PAULINE I've spoken to Dr. Egerman. He explained he's got to keep you locked up until the New Year, otherwise you'd be in trouble with the police, and your sentence for having tried to kill me would be altered to at least six years' forced labor. How about that?

ÅKERBLOM Yes, yes, yes . . .

PAULINE But on the first of January Egerman can discharge you—on probation, as it's called—provided I look after you. So, you'll be in my hands and I'll damned well keep you on the straight and narrow, my sweet boy.

ÅKERBLOM You're not to swear like that, Pauline. It doesn't suit you.

PAULINE I am a qualified physiotherapist and am wholly independent; no one is to tell me what words I perchance have the right to use. D'you hear me?

ÅKERBLOM Yes.

PAULINE Is that quite clear?

ÅKERBLOM Yes!

PAULINE Then I'll go on.

PAULINE takes a large brown envelope out of her briefcase.

PAULINE A reply has come from the Royal Patent Office.

ÅKERBLOM With my application returned.

PAULINE You may well say that. The Royal Patent Office writes: "Your application cannot be granted as what you call your 'cinematocamera' was constructed in 1896 by R. W. Paul, who soon saw that his invention, the 'theatrograph,' would have no practical application. However, the world patent still stands (Paris C.D.C. no: 18963875). For the Royal Patent Office. Signed, Stockholm, the fourteenth of October, Q. Nilsson, Patents Officer." Stamped and franked. There you are.

PAULINE tosses the papers onto ÅKERBLOM's stomach as he lies on his bed.

PAULINE It cost seven kronor, fifty-five öre to redeem this document.

ÅKERBLOM Did you perhaps think I'd be miserable?

PAULINE Well, you weren't exactly pleased.

ÅKERBLOM Ah, my dear Pauline, that bright idea is already a long way back in my life.

ÅKERBLOM sits himself on the edge of the bed, tears the papers in two above his head, scatters them, and walks over to PAULINE.

ÅKERBLOM The "CINEMATOCAMERA" is dead, long live the "Live Talking Picture." THE LIVING TALKING PICTURE with the emphasis on "living." La cinématographie vivante parlante! Away with scratchy gramophone records! Away with fumbling mechanics and wretched film clips of, at the most, four minutes.

PAULINE What's the matter, Carl? Your face has gone so red, flaring up with pride!

ÅKERBLOM Here you see the projector in its sound-insulated chamber. Here is the white screen. The picture is outlined on the white screen. A beautiful woman turns her languishing gaze to the audience and whispers with sensual, moist lips: "I love you, Bertrand!" No distracting text! No delay! You, the spectator, hear the lovely whisper. It strikes your heightened emotions at the very moment it is pronounced. The miracle is a fact. Cinematography, man's greatest invention after the splendid wheel, is perfected. Like all really great innovations, it is a foolishly simple construction. I'm not ashamed to call it brilliant.

PAULINE And how is it to function?

ÅKERBLOM The white screen on which our heroine's face is projected is transparent. Behind the screen is an actress. She speaks into a microphone and says her lines at the same moment as the picture's heroine says them. The microphone picks up the words and carries them via an amplifier and a loudspeaker to the audience. Voilá, la cinématographie parlante!

PAULINE I really do think you've created something revolutionary.

ÅKERBLOM We'll be acting in a cinema film, entirely according to this new method, and we'll conquer the world.

PAULINE And what is the film about?

ÅKERBLOM Hmm . . . hmm . . . It'll be a gripping cinematography, I assure you. Lots of music.

PAULINE Music?

ÅKERBLOM A pianino[5] behind the screen. And you playing . . . Schubert symphonies, arranged for piano.

PAULINE Why Schubert?

ÅKERBLOM Because this cinematography is about Schubert, you silly cow.

PAULINE About Schubert?

ÅKERBLOM It's about brother Franz! And his love deal with the young Countess Mizzi, who took her own life by drowning herself in the Danube in the late autumn of 1908.

PAULINE But didn't Schubert die in 1828?

ÅKERBLOM What the hell does that matter? She . . . a poor prostitute, just a child. He . . . a genius.

PAULINE Wasn't she a countess?

ÅKERBLOM If you're going to quibble over words and waste time on inessentials, then you can go to hell. What I need is pens and writing paper, a lot of writing paper—of good quality.

PAULINE But Carl . . .

ÅKERBLOM Let your young heart be enthused, my darling. Just for once. Just . . . for . . . once . . .

PAULINE starts to cry.

PAULINE I want to, so very much.

ÅKERBLOM This is the future, Pauline.

PAULINE But actors cost money.

ÅKERBLOM Trifles! Who'll be Schubert? I myself, in all modesty. I'll be a Schubert no one hitherto has ever thought of or seen. Not even himself. And you? You are created for Mizzi!

PAULINE appalled.

PAULINE Me? But I was meant to be playing the piano.

ÅKERBLOM When you're not speaking, you play the piano.

PAULINE Am I supposed to be a prostitute? What do you think my aunts will say about that?

ÅKERBLOM I've already told you that Mizzi was a virgin.

PAULINE No, you never said that.

ÅKERBLOM Didn't I? Well, yes, Mizzi was a virgin.

PAULINE Then how can she have been a prostitute?

ÅKERBLOM What foolish, trivial questions! I've just read in the newspaper that the film industry is in difficulties, that the problems are primarily artistic rather than financial—new ideas produce new money! I see lovely, colorful, brilliant pictures, faces, limbs, movements, and then music.

PAULINE hugs and smothers ÅKERBLOM in kisses.

PAULINE Sometimes I wonder why I love you as I do, Carl Åkerblom. You're fat; you're bloated; your hair's beginning to grow horribly gray; you're not kind; you've even tried to kill me. You've deceived me twice during our engagement. I don't understand what other ladies see in you that's so attractive. No, as I said. When clear-sightedness afflicts me, and that quite often happens nowadays, then I don't understand, don't understand why I actually . . . love you! But now, as you stand there in your . . . in your, in your . . . holding forth on this "living talking film" . . . no, don't say anything . . . and all that we're going to do together. Well, then I just want to cry and fall to my knees and perhaps even kiss your hands.

ÅKERBLOM is moved and confused. PAULINE sits on the floor.

PAULINE Come, let me embrace you, Åkerblom.

ÅKERBLOM lies down on the floor with his head in her arms, against her breast.

NURSE STELLA You may go in.

The door is unlocked and OSVALD VOGLER enters cautiously, and crouches on the floor.

VOGLER My dear Åkerblom . . .

ÅKERBLOM May I introduce my fiancée?

VOGLER Delighted. Once I was home, I longed to be back. As you can see, I have insisted on institution attire. One has to . . . Well, my wife has finally accepted. She has wept all day, but is now happy. Shall we drink a toast?

EMMA VOGLER has also entered though we have not seen her until now, pouring out champagne into four tin mugs. They sit in a row on the bed.

VOGLER What do you say about a joint project? Against chaos and dissolution?

EMMA VOGLER signs.

PAULINE Forgive me for asking, but what is your wife saying?

VOGLER She keeps repeating: "We love all of us! We love all of us!"

EMMA VOGLER kisses ÅKERBLOM and then PAULINE—laughter and kissing in rapid succession.

ÅKERBLOM A minute ago I related to my fiancée a project of global significance.

VOGLER A joint project?

ÅKERBLOM Exceptionally joint! Cheers!

ALL FOUR clash mugs.

ACT II

ÅKERBLOM The Å.V. Film Company Limited has the honor to present the first and only live talking film in the history of the world.

Alternate lines FILM POSTER[6] read by ÅKERBLOM and VOGLER:

ÅKERBLOM THE JOYS OF A LADY OF THE NIGHT

VOGLER CINE-DRAMA IN THREE ACTS

ÅKERBLOM BY AND FEATURING

VOGLER CARL ÅKERBLOM, MIA FALK, PAULINE THIBAULT, OSVALD VOGLER, AND MANY OTHERS

ÅKERBLOM This gripping cinematograph drama takes place in Vienna in the nineteenth century; its subject: The passionate love between the genius, Franz Schubert, and the lady of the night, Mizzi Veith.

VOGLER SPLENDID SETS, BRILLIANT MUSIC

ÅKERBLOM GREAT ACTING

VOGLER FROM THE WORLD PRESS: "Nobody left unmoved . . ."—*Molde District Chronicle*

Scene 1

The snow comes swirling down and the poster, which the wind has blown askew on the notice board of the Grånäs[7] Good Templar Hall, is pinned back into place by ALMA BERGLUND. *She goes up the steps and enters. Inside, she fills the stove from the coal hopper, then swiftly stirs it about with a poker before disappearing behind the stage.*

The Good Templar building in Grånäs was put up many years ago during the intoxicating passion for teetotalism that engulfed the area. Later on, the building fell into decay without anyone worrying much about it. It was strategically situated, close to the Snickarbo Railway way-station, before the track turns inland toward the forest country. The River Gimå, rarely frozen over, rushes by below the building. The worn, wooden building, painted russet-red, is spacious and seats almost two hundred. One end is taken up by a stage with curtain and footlights. There are eight windows and if necessary they can be blacked out with blinds. The tilt-seats are wooden. The walls are adorned with glass bracket lamps in the shape of bluebells and equipped with carbon filament lights, below which are framed enlarged photographs from what, in retrospect, now seems fossilized activity in the service of teetotalism. The backcloth of the stage is a birch-wood opening out onto a quiet lake—beyond it, hills in a blueing light. Under the roofing hang three flats depicting summer clouds damaged by damp. At the back there is a stove fueled with wood and coal. It glows and pings. Above the stove is a washing line hung with gear of varying gender. There is a cot with no mattress, its foot-end turned toward the source of heat; under a gray horse blanket, OSVALD VOGLER *is asleep, motionless as if dead. In the middle of the stage, in the pale winter light from the high windows, some of them boarded up,* PAULINE THIBAULT *is standing in her petticoat, a man's overcoat, and curlers, ironing. A second iron is heating on top of the stove, alongside a saucepan of broth.*

The portable cinematograph apparatus is on its stand, by the foot-lights, and, beside it, a tower of black film cartons, which have just been unpacked.

Apart from that, the stage is cluttered with furniture from the upper floor, a red velvet pile sofa, an armchair covered in worn leather, a few wooden chairs, and a narrow table with carved legs. A tall cracked wall mirror is leaning in a corner.

The company's opened and unopened luggage is scattered here and there. Two lamps with green shades hang from the ceiling, competing on equal terms with the rapidly failing daylight. A few rickety sheds can be seen through the window. The snow is now falling heavily and silently.

MIA FALK is sitting on a stool. She is a short, plump twenty-year-old, wrapped in a shabby fur coat. Her cheeks are rosy, her mouth small and shapely; her glances are of cold loveliness.

PETRUS LANDAHL is up on a ladder near the curtain, trying to hang the screen on dangling ropes. He is the local carpentry teacher, his eyes watery, the lids drooping; he has forgotten to shave, his beard unkempt; his hair is thick and dark, his cheeks pale. Occasionally he coughs cautiously into a handkerchief already spotted with blood. He is wearing dark clothes; a woolen cardigan is just visible under his jacket.

MRS. BERGLUND, well wrapped up in a fur coat, pushes her way in through a side door, hurries over to the stove, and pours out a mug of steaming broth, which she then cautiously slurps down.

MRS. BERGLUND Good day to you, Miss Thibault. Good day, Miss Falk.

PAULINE Good day, Mrs. Berglund, how are sales going?

MRS. BERGLUND Eleven tickets.

PAULINE Oh! Is that all?

MRS. BERGLUND Ain't too bad, I'll have you know, considering how remote we are.

PAULINE And the weather, of course.

MRS. BERGLUND Yes—and the weather. Mr. Landahl, would you please put up a new poster? The one out there's all in pieces due to the wind.

PETRUS Right you are, Mrs. Berglund.

MRS. BERGLUND It's going to get colder toward evening and a storm's due from up north and worse snow. So people are going to have trouble getting here. Hasn't Åkerblom turned up?

PAULINE No. He's probably gone for a walk through the village.

MRS. BERGLUND Yes, Grånäs is where he lived as a child, ain't it? I'll be in the box office, if I'm needed, like.

Exit MRS. BERGLUND.

PAULINE Stenbjörka, Storforsen, Videvik, Mörktjärn[8] . . . and then Grånäs, of course.

MIA It hasn't exactly been a triumphant procession, has it?

PAULINE Haven't you had your food and lodging? Haven't you had your fifteen kronor a week, dead on time?

MIA But I'm tired of . . .

PAULINE You can leave. I won't stop you. Just say what you want, but don't *whine*!

PETRUS I've seen *The Joys of a Lady of the Night* sixteen times and it's the artistic experience of my life, that and seeing *The Conspiracy of the Batavians* at the National Museum of Fine Arts in Stockholm. You'll remember your time here, Miss Falk, believe you me. You'll remember it and be grateful.

MIA Kiss me slowly . . . on my arse.

PAULINE puts the iron down so brusquely on the upturned plate that it breaks.

PAULINE Just you listen, Mia Falk! I've tolerated you long enough. I've seen you in bed with Åkerblom and said nothing. I've heard you kissing and cuddling, and I've not complained.

I've tolerated your insults and swallowed your humiliating allusions without protest. But have you given it a thought, Mia Falk, that there comes a time when nothing in the whole world is of any importance compared to the enjoyment of pressing this red hot iron into your nasty little mug!

MIA Hell, I was only joking.

PAULINE Thought as much.

MIA *I* can't help it if Åkerblom chases me like a hornet.

PAULINE *returns to her ironing*.

PAULINE I'm sure you can't.

MIA Well, then.

PETRUS *has fetched new film posters*.

PETRUS It's snowing really heavily now. And the wind's got up. This is what it sounds like when a storm blows in off the heath.

VOGLER *suddenly wakes up*.

VOGLER I must be off to my lecture.

PAULINE Calm down! It doesn't start for two hours.

PETRUS *pauses, looking at the projector*.

PAULINE Petrus, are you going to get the screen up?

PETRUS Yes, yes. Just waiting for Åkerblom to come and help.

PAULINE You do know how to crank the cinematograph?

PETRUS Well, I don't know . . . well, yes, I think I can.

PAULINE But you can load?

PETRUS Well, no . . . yes, I think so.

PAULINE For that matter, you don't have to be able to, because I'll come and help you in the intervals. There'll be two intervals and then you're to put the house lights on and sell sweets. In the meantime I'll reload.

PETRUS *coughs*.

PAULINE How's your cough?

PETRUS Not to worry—everyone in Grånäs has a cold. The children snivel, the parents clear their throats, and the elderly have temperatures . . . All you can do is: accept and adjust, as the vicar said.

PAULINE But, Petrus, how can you . . . ?

PETRUS . . . be here today? Hush! I'm playing truant. Do you think, Miss, I ought to give up an experience for duty's sake? Experience is the inquiring mind's only real duty.

PAULINE Well, perhaps . . . I must finish the ironing.

PETRUS And I must put up a new poster outside the entrance. The old one's blown down.

MIA I've got toothache.

PAULILNE is silent.

MIA Oh, to hell with all this.

PAULINE does not reply.

MIA I'll get a train to Falun. The goods train stops at Grånäs at three o'clock. I'll make it if I leave straightaway.

PAULINE is still silent.

MIA This tooth hurts and I think it's loose. The doctor said he'd have to cut the gum and clean it up. It didn't ache at the time, so I said no. Has the cat got your tongue, Pauline?

PAULINE Probably.

MIA Then I'll be off, then.

MIA gets up from the stool, sweeps her shabby fur around her, and strides over to PAULINE.

PAULINE No farewell kiss?

MIA and PAULINE hug, kissing each other.

MIA So you're not angry at my leaving, eh?

PAULINE No, no, Mia, I'm not angry. I'm just sad beyond all reason, and tired. Go now, Mia, before someone sees you leaving.

PAULINE embraces MIA and kisses her on the mouth. MIA returns her kiss and whimpers a little in PAULINE's arms.

PAULINE You ought to see a dentist as soon as you can; it smells a bit peculiar.

MIA It was for your sake I joined you on this adventure.

PAULINE Oh, Christ! The money!

PAULINE hurries over to her handbag and takes out a few notes.

MIA Can't we both run off and leave the old men and the whole caboodle?

PAULINE Take this. And go. At once.

MIA stuffs the money into her pocket, sweeps a scarf around her head, and grasps the suitcase she never unpacked. She goes out through a narrow door in the end wall. Snow blows in. PAULINE sits down and lights a cigarette. OSVALD VOGLER wakes up.

VOGLER The probable does not exist, since it postulates the existence of the improbable. Consequently the probable cannot be accepted, since it presupposes what we call the improbable. That's it . . . yes.

VOGLER lies down again. ÅKERBLOM enters, cheerful. The snow howls in as the door opens.

ÅKERBLOM Good afternoon, my Paulina-Lilywhite! Is there anything edible?

PAULINE Broth and some bread.

ÅKERBLOM Ah! How is Osvald?

PAULINE I don't know.

PAULINE brushes snow off ÅKERBLOM and straightens his hair.

ÅKERBLOM A good old hangover.

PAULINE Since his wife left he's got worse.

ÅKERBLOM On the contrary! Now that he is drinking uninhibitedly he's become quite coherent.

PAULINE Well, he is seventy-eight.

ÅKERBLOM What have you done with Mia?

PAULINE I'm not really sure.

ÅKERBLOM laughs.

ÅKERBLOM What kind of tone of voice was that?

PAULINE You seem to be in an enviably good mood, anyhow. Where've you been all day?

ÅKERBLOM Grånäs is my childhood country—perhaps you knew that. Papa built a handsome summer place a mile or two from here, halfway up a mountain. I roamed around, I just roamed around. I took the forest road up to the house, wondering whether anyone lived there. There were no shutters on the windows, but otherwise it was all dark and locked up, footprints and wheel ruts in the snow. Yes, it was almost mysterious, the river flowing along, deep as it is down there, dark and gleaming, the snow falling, falling; and sometimes the wind blew and the twin-trunked birch swung its gleaming branches . . .

PAULINE interrupts.

PAULINE Mrs. Berglund came by and said she's sold eleven tickets.

ÅKERBLOM Landahl! Landahl!

PETRUS Here, Mr. Åkerblom.

ÅKERBLOM We must get the projector in position.

PETRUS Exactly what I was about to suggest.

ÅKERBLOM Kind of you to help, Mr. Landahl, now that our labor force has been decimated. Where *is* Mia?

PAULINE It's up to you to keep track of her.

ÅKERBLOM and PETRUS start lugging the projector.

ÅKERBLOM We must position the projector up in the gallery, then we'll run the electric cable down here to the footlights and put stronger fuses in the fusebox.

PETRUS The loudspeakers are in position. I just need to connect the microphones.

ÅKERBLOM unscrews the fuses.

ÅKERBLOM Right! Now for strengthening the fuses so they don't blow as they did in Besna and Lännheden,[9] when we started the arc light. Mr. Landahl, have you got two penny coins?

PETRUS Well . . . I suppose so.

ÅKERBLOM puts the coins into the back of the fuse sockets.

ÅKERBLOM Then that goes there, and that one there.

PETRUS But, Mr. Åkerblom! That's illegal and dangerous.

ÅKERBLOM Art knows no laws. For art everything is dangerous. Let's get the projector to the front of the gallery.

ÅKERBLOM and PETRUS return to lugging the projector through the vestibule and up the stairs to the gallery.

PETRUS Yes, but people usually like sitting in the front row of the gallery.

ÅKERBLOM It can't be helped. We must close off the gallery. That's the fire regulations, Mr. Landahl. Dangerous toys, these! We must put the fire extinguisher up here in the gallery as well.

PETRUS Already taken care of, Mr. Åkerblom.

ÅKERBLOM Nitrate film explodes like gunpowder, you know, Mr. Landahl. It's bloody inflammable.

PETRUS I know—just as I read in the paper the other day: nineteen cinemas burned down last year in Italy. One hundred seventeen people lost their lives.

PAULINE is seated at a small wooden table. Wearing a pince-nez, and having found a lead pencil, she is adding up columns and sums with silent lip movements, chewing the pencil and counting the money in the cash box. The wind is rising, the dark gathering outside. Loud thumps assault the outer door. The door is yanked open by a man in a gray greatcoat and fur hat to reveal a small lady in an elegant fur coat, a muff, galoshes, and a sable hat.

It is ANNA ÅKERBLOM. At this stage in life, she would be sixty-six. The little figure holds herself well, has a round pale face, a determined double chin, gray-blue eyes, elegant snub nose, and a "mouth not for kissing, but for giving orders."

ANNA Jansson, wait by the car.

PAULINE has stood up, but does not step forward to meet the visitor.

ANNA I am Carl's stepmother.

PAULINE And I, his fiancée.

ANNA As Carl is under guardianship, I consider such a state of betrothal to be somewhat doubtful.

PAULINE "Adult male may without consultation or permission from his guardian enter into engagement, betrothal, or any comparable noneconomic undertaking."

ANNA May I be seated?

PAULINE Of course. I'm sorry. It's a bit of a muddle here, but we've been delayed by the snowstorm.

ANNA So there's to be a . . . what's it called?

PAULINE A cinema performance, perhaps?

VOGLER wakes up.

VOGLER Excuse me, dear ladies. Nature calls.

PAULINE Osvald, don't forget to put something on!

VOGLER waves in refusal.

VOGLER Yes, yes, yes, yes.

ANNA Professor Vogler, I imagine. Won't you sit down, young lady?

PAULINE Of course. I'm afraid I've nothing to offer you.

ANNA I haven't come here to have coffee.

PAULINE I can understand that. Well?

ANNA gets out a letter.

ANNA In the name of honesty, I ought to inform you, Miss Thibault, that Carl's guardian has written to Professor Vogler's wife, as we are aware that the professor's wife has financed this enterprise. The other week, he received a detailed reply to his letter, in which the professor's wife says that on her husband's urgent request, she has withdrawn from all commitments and that she knows nothing of the future destiny of the project. In a postscript, she mentions that Mr. Åkerblom and Professor Vogler have between them run through seventy-two thousand riksdalers[10] and that Miss Thibault is now held to be responsible for all the organization and financing.

ANNA ÅKERBLOM folds up the letter from which she has, from time to time, been quoting and returns it to the interior of her muff. PAULINE lights a cigarette.

PAULINE I would be grateful if you would be kind enough, Mrs. Åkerblom, to account for the reason for your visit.

ANNA By all means, Miss Thibault. I have come to take my mad stepson home.

PAULINE What if I say no?

ANNA Perhaps I may say that I feel a reluctant admiration for your person, Miss Thibault. In addition, we have something in common, and that is our love for the boy Carl. We love him, it's as simple as that. When I became his stepmother, he was twenty-six but still a child, a highly neglected child, I would have it, badly treated by his friends and his older brothers. He was frightened and kind and industrious, terribly cleanly and ambitious and anxiously pedantic. The difficulty, the great difficulty was that he was afflicted with attacks of rage.

ANNA smiles.

ANNA He once actually broke my nose.

PAULINE Why, Mrs. Åkerblom, are you telling me all these things that I already know?

ANNA You know only what my stepson happens to have told you.

PAULINE That's true.

PAULINE lights another cigarette.

ANNA Would you mind not smoking, Miss Thibault. It embarrasses me.

PAULINE Forgive me.

PAULINE stubs out the cigarette on a plate of bread-and-butter remains.

ANNA I care for that careless old child. I want to give him a little security.

PAULINE And so do I.

ANNA When he realizes his grandiose project has gone the way of the world . . .

PAULINE Yes. Well?

ANNA No.

PAULINE If it's any consolation to you, Mrs. Åkerblom, if it's any consolation, then Carl and I are fairly unhappy. We quarrel over the slightest thing. He lies to me all the time, although he doesn't have to lie. That week in February—when we were filming *The Joys of a Lady of the Night*—was a grandiose hell. I was to play Mizzi; that was the leading female part, but then he caught sight of a young actress called Mia Falk. She seduced him and then I was out of the picture. It took less than twenty minutes. And Professor Vogler, who was to write the script, made changes and had new lines every day, and he and Carl and Mia ganged up together against me and what was I to do? I liked all *three* of them. I do believe I've got some sherry in my bag.

PAULINE gets sherry and glasses out of a bag.

PAULINE And the money poured out. At the time that was no problem, as Mrs. Vogler realized her beloved husband was happier and healthier than he'd been for years. So she paid. And then we winked in conspiration at each other and I assured them that once the masterpiece was finished, the money would be retrieved. But then one film company after another said no. And there we were, with *The Joys of a Lady of the Night*, the very first, and hitherto unique, living speaking film in world history. Then we said to each other, let's go on tour. We'll rent premises, by degrees. And one day, we'll be *visible*. And *then*: success will come. But Vogler suddenly wanted to send his kind wife packing and so she went home with the money. So now things are as they are, Mrs. Åkerblom.

ANNA Perhaps the time's come to call a halt?

PAULINE I've still got six hundred and fifty-three kronor and seventy öre in the cash box.

ANNA And how long will that six hundred and fifty-three kronor last, if I may ask?

PAULINE Three, perhaps four performances. That depends on the takings.

Silence. ANNA appears to be pondering what has been said.

ANNA Would it be tactless to ask how you met my stepson, Miss Thibault?

PAULINE Hasn't he told you anything?

ANNA He's said many things. Someone had "opened his eyes." His previous life had been "an illusion," and so on. When I wanted to know more, he became very stern and in the end asked me to stay away. I cannot deny that I was distressed.

PAULINE Do have some more sherry.

ANNA Thank you.

PAULINE refills both glases.

PAULINE I met him one August evening two years ago. He was singing in the University Choir and I was playing the piano part in Brahms's Liebeslieder waltzes. At the party afterward, Carl at once started being troublesome. Someone praised Leibniz and Carl was furious and started quoting Schopenhauer: "In compassion we gain higher freedom, as we free ourselves from selfish volition and feel fellowship with all the suffering in the world." His fine, beautiful eyes were black with rage and that fat, clumsy, shy, anxious creature . . . well, I looked at him and . . . Then there was a terrible to-do. He got hold of a cheese knife and slashed his antagonist's cheek so that the blood squirted . . .

ANNA That'll do. I remember.

PAULINE He ended up in the asylum and I wrote to him and got lovely replies full of poems and drawings. Then I started going to see him, and . . . we got engaged, secretly, of course.

ANNA And he tried to kill you.

PAULINE You could say that, I suppose.

ANNA And now we're here. In Grånäs and six hundred and fifty-three kronor from the end.

PAULINE More or less, yes.

ANNA Then what?

PAULINE I am indifferent, Mrs. Åkerblom.

ANNA It doesn't worry you?

PAULINE I find I am beyond the kind of worry that you speak of, Mrs. Åkerblom.

ANNA How remarkable.

PAULINE Is that a compliment?

ANNA opens her handbag and produces three hundred-kronor notes, which she puts down beside the bottle of sherry.

ANNA Might this be of some use, perhaps?

PAULINE No, thank you.

ANNA Not?

Short pause. ANNA puts the notes back.

ANNA I understand.

PAULINE I must ask you to leave now, Mrs. Åkerblom.

ANNA Must you?

PAULINE Please forgive my lack of courtesy, but I wish to prevent a meeting.

ANNA gets up.

ANNA Farewell, Miss Thibault.

PAULINE Farewell, Mrs. Åkerblom.

ANNA ÅKERBLOM moves toward the door, but stops, and stands still, her head lowered.

ANNA Oh dear . . .

PAULINE What is it?

ANNA sits herself down on a stool by the door.

ANNA My husband died six years ago. He had been ill for several years, but it was lonely, in the immediate vicinity, if I can put it that way. Then my daughter married—that was a misfortune. Everything was . . . is deplorable.

PAULINE Then your son died?

ANNA He was killed in an air accident. He was a meteorologist and was studying the formation of thunderstorms.

PAULINE Yes.

ANNA Since then I seem to get so tired.

PAULINE Was it Carl's illness?

ANNA Not the first time, nor the second, but what happened to you, Miss Thibault?

PAULINE I knew about his jealousy, and it was my fault.

ANNA This is what it's like with Carl and his stepmother. He rests on my heart. And I neither want to, nor am able to, tip him off. When I joined the household, I was about the same age as you are now, Miss Thibault. On the very first day, he curled up above my heart . . . just here . . .

ANNA gestures with a clenched hand.

ANNA . . . and there he stayed. Sometimes it got rather sore.

PAULINE And now I've taken over . . . the responsibility.

ANNA Perhaps you think I'm jealous, Miss Thibault?

PAULINE Is that so terribly inconceivable?

ANNA It's perhaps a little naïve.

PAULINE But I love him.

ANNA A life catastrophe does not submit to persuasion, Miss Thibault. An emotion here, a passion there, a hospital, medicaments, promises, death, friendly relations, solicitude, discipline, "love" if you will. All those are chance circumstances, thin threads . . . I'm just tired.

ANNA rises.

ANNA Tired of waiting.

PAULINE Won't you be coming to tonight's performance, Mrs. Åkerblom?

ANNA I shan't, but my daughter will—Karin, Carl's half sister, who happens to be staying, with her two small sons. Carl and Karin are very attached to each other. Good-bye, Miss Thibault.

PAULINE curtsies. ANNA opens the door and disappears into the snow and darkness. PAULINE pours more coal into the stove. She hears a cough. It is VOGLER hidden in a red armchair, wet through.

PAULINE Osvald!

VOGLER Yes. Forgive me. I got a bit chilled.

PAULINE Why are you sitting here, Osvald?

VOGLER I didn't want to disturb you.

PAULINE Oh, no! Come on and let's find you something to drink, Osvald, and then get you tucked into bed.

ÅKERBLOM Switch on the current, brother Landahl! Just switch on! Don't be afraid. The worst that can happen is that Grånäs Good Templar Hall gets blown to smithereens!

A sharp bright square of light shines through the curtain. CARL ÅK-ERBLOM *steps into the patch of light. He is cheerful.*

ÅKERBLOM Splendid, Mr. Landahl, the pennies did the trick.

PETRUS is up in the gallery.

PETRUS They did and all, but we're near the limit—I just crank and I crank . . . (*talking to himself*) One, two, three. One, two, three . . .

ÅKERBLOM You'd better come down now.

PETRUS Right. I'll switch off and be down.

ÅKERBLOM (*to Pauline*) Have you seen Mia? Where's she got to?

PAULINE You'd better look for her.

ÅKERBLOM Mama was here.

PAULINE It was just as well you kept away.

ÅKERBLOM I do not want an account of her visit, thank you.

PAULINE You'll not be getting one.

Scene 2

The light on the curtain has gone out and PETRUS LANDAHL *makes his entrance on stage. He is brimming with energy.*

ÅKERBLOM Ah, there you are! Now let's get that curtain up!

PETRUS Right, Mr. Åkerblom. Now all we have to do is hoist the sail of the vessel that is to take us to the boundless continent of mysterious shadows.

ÅKERBLOM and PETRUS pull on two ropes, hoisting the screen. PAULINE plays a chord or two on the pianino. ÅKERBLOM starts mounting the microphone, as PAULINE wipes the ivories with a cloth.

ÅKERBLOM Now you've got to find Mia.

PAULINE She's left.

ÅKERBLOM She's *left?*

PAULINE She's left, yes.

ÅKERBLOM Oh, she has, has she? Well, that's hardly a national disaster . . .

PAULINE You take it so calmly?

ÅKERBLOM We can actually well do without her, and save money, too. She was expensive to run, the little tart.

PAULINE What are we to do then?

ÅKERBLOM You can take over the part of Mizzi.

PAULINE I don't know the lines.

ÅKERBLOM laughs.

ÅKERBLOM Nonsense! Of course you know them. You can read them from the script.

PAULINE In the dark? On the stage?

ÅKERBLOM Someone can hold a torch, for Christ's sake!

PAULINE And who's to hold the torch if you're playing Schubert, I'm playing Mizzi, Osvald's playing the other parts, and Petrus is cranking the projector?

ÅKERBLOM God, what nagging!

MRS. BERGLUND turns up by the footlights. She has been home and has put on her Sunday best and curled her fringe. She has brought a basket containing two thermoses and a paper bag filled with some-thing.

MRS. BERGLUND It's time to let the audience in, isn't it?

ÅKERBLOM Yes! Let the audience in, Mr. Landahl, and illumi-nate the premises!

PETRUS Aye, aye, Cap'n!

PETRUS goes into the vestibule. He switches on the house lights and then stands in the entrance to collect the ticket stubs.

PETRUS Right then. You're all very welcome, just step inside!

MRS. BERGLUND opens the pass door a bit so she and PAULINE can peep at the audience.

MRS. BERGLUND That's the teacher from Frostnäs, Märta Lund-berg, who got here on skis, but the Reverend Ericsson's not coming because he's got a cold. Then there's Mrs. Persson—it was me who invited her. She never goes out to anything since her husband committed suicide last autumn. He was a brooder. Algot Frövik has such trouble with his joints, he's almost an invalid and it's specially bad when the cold sets in. But if it's a question of culture, nothing'll stop him coming. It appears Mr. Larsson, the chief superintendent, has made his way here and that's certainly no frequent event, but he's not here in the course of duty—he's intimate with Hanna, and that's a real se-cret, but everyone knows and thinks they might well make a pair as Larsson's been a widower for five years. And that's Fre-drik Blom; he was the cantor in Frostnäs and then he nigh on drank himself to death and he's still here living on some small sickness benefit and is doing research into chorales from Skat-tungbyn. And then there's little Mrs. Bergman, Åkerblom's sister.

The SPECTATORS are now seated. PETRUS pours more coal into the stove. PAULINE wakes VOGLER, gently shaking him.

PAULINE Osvald, Osvald . . .

VOGLER throws off the horse blanket and sits up, very much half asleep.

VOGLER Oh, has the time come? We're off?

ÅKERBLOM gives him a shot of schnapps in a small jam jar.

PAULINE The audience has already come and we're to start at any moment.

VOGLER I've forgotten what I'm to say.

ÅKERBLOM You enter in front of the curtain and welcome the audience and then you say that Grånäs, don't forget GRÅNÄS, is at this moment the center of the artistic expansion of cinematography.

VOGLER Yes, yes . . . There's no need to go on so. I know my part.

ÅKERBLOM Yes. Good. Right.

PAULINE How are you feeling?

VOGLER I'm a bit dizzy. I might go so far as to say that the room is spinning.

PAULINE Will you be all right?

VOGLER Yes, yes, yes.

The narrow pass door, stage left, is yanked open. A woman in an elegant fur coat pushes her way in. She laughs, closing the door behind her. ÅKERBLOM hugs her vigorously.

ÅKERBLOM Oh, Karrie! Dearest little sis, have you come to see your brother's "spectacle?" That really makes me happy.

KARIN BERGMAN The boys have been poorly all autumn so the doctor ordered a change of air. We got up here six weeks ago with Mummy. It's all so wonderful. You must come and see us.

ÅKERBLOM I'm not alone.

KARIN BERGMAN I know. Where is your Pauline?

PAULINE Here's his Pauline! Good evening. Be our guest.

KARIN BERGMAN Thank you! What a lovely dress!

PAULINE Well, it's not exactly eighteenth century.

ÅKERBLOM Can't you come back stage afterward and say good-bye, even if you didn't think much of our performance?

PETRUS comes in through the door, looking stressed.

PETRUS Can't we get going? It's a quarter past eight. And as far as I can see, all the audience is in.

PETRUS turns to KARIN BERGMAN.

PETRUS Good day, or rather good evening. May I offer you a hand, Madam, and I'll find you an excellent seat. Just bang the gong, Mr. Åkerblom, when we're to begin, then I'll know when to put out the lights and start cranking the projector along.

ÅKERBLOM Right.

PETRUS goes into the vestibule and switches off the lights. Suddenly he leans forward, grimacing in pain; he takes a step or two forward and then falls to his knees, coughing blood. He gets out a handkerchief and wipes his mouth; then he quickly gets up and hurries up the stairs.

Enter VOGLER down stage. He is dazzled by the glare of the gelatined footlights.

VOGLER Most honored audience, in the terrible caves of primeval times, primeval people assembled and in an unfathomable excess of desire they painted forms on the damp walls, or carved figures, or hammered out the most amazing ornaments. Through mighty storms, along inaccessible paths, and in every conceivable discomfort, other people came to look at those painted images, those carved figures. Or to feel the polished amber in their hands. Can one be anything but moved, I ask, but that is a rhetorical question. I am not even sure that any one of you present in front of me or behind this soiled cloth grasps the greatness of this evening's . . .

PAULINE reaches out through the curtain and gets ahold of VOGLER's hand.

VOGLER Eh? What is it?

With gentle determination PAULINE pulls VOGLER off into the wings.

ÅKERBLOM strikes the gong.

PAULINE sits down at the piano and plays the main theme from the first movement of Schubert's ninth symphony, arranged for piano. We, still up on the stage, read, mirror-imaged, the caption:

YNAPMOC MLIFEVÅ

then we read from the auditorium:

PRESENTS

and, after a major racking adjustment by the projectionist:

A TALKING CINEMA DRAMA

and:

TO WIT

and, from the stage again, in much larger letters:

THGIN EHT FO YDAL A FO SYOJ

and, smaller letters again:

YB

then, large letters filling the screen:

MOLBREKÅ LRAC

The music continues as the following captions are projected:

A splendid spring day

and:

Franz Schubert lies on his impoverished deathbed

A close-up of FRANZ SCHUBERT (ÅKERBLOM) on his sickbed emerges, a bed of pain and humiliation. You can see that he is feverish, his hair untidy and his throat glistening with sweat. Now we see the whole sickroom. The pianist brings the music to a natural finish as a door at the back opens and a lovely and noticeably well-dressed young woman (PAULINE) floats over to the bed and falls to her knees. Close-up of SCHUBERT.

ÅKERBLOM—*SCHUBERT* You came after all, my darling Mizzi!

And the voice is real! It is ÅKERBLOM whispering behind the suspended screen. He moves close to the square microphone and says those compelling words: "You came after all, my darling Mizzi!" PAULINE has left the piano and hurried over to the other microphone and now Mizzi's tearstained face fills the whole canvas as she whispers:

PAULINE—*MIZZI* Whatever happens, you must know that I love you, my own Franz.

PAULINE whispers beautifully into the microphone and the loudspeaker transmits her gentle tone of voice to the little congregation in Grånäs Good Templar Hall. The sick man proffers a bundle of handwritten music, and says:

ÅKERBLOM—*SCHUBERT* Play for me, my dearest, play for me!

PAULINE leaves her microphone and sits down at the piano to the right of the proscenium. Another close-up of SCHUBERT. He closes his eyes, his previously untidy hair has now settled, the glistening sweat at his throat has gone, as have the stains on his nightshirt. He closes his eyes and a smile brightens his ravaged (by makeup) features. MIZZI, i.e., PAULINE backstage, plays the second movement of the ninth symphony. A caption:

In his last moments the maestro listens to this music, hitherto unheard.

The emotion is total in Grånäs Good Templar Hall, savaged by icy winds from the heath beyond the river.

Then this happens: First a bang, an explosion, a shot. Then a drawn-out hissing noise. The beautiful sepia-tinted picture, illuminated by a sun, flickers and goes out. The house, stage and all, goes pitch black; the only light there is comes from the cavernous, glowing eyes of the stove, but that's not even enough to grope about in. PETRUS *stops cranking. Incontrovertible darkness has descended from the snow-laden heavens to envelop the Good Templar Hall. It could not be darker. Moreover, the silence is paralyzing. Some members of the audience rise; others light matches; then a shout:*

MÄRTA LUNDBERG I think the vestibule is on fire!

ALGOT FRÖVIK The fusebox is on fire, that's what it is.

PETRUS Don't panic! I've got a torch! I'll get the fire extinguisher!

PETRUS *switches the torch on and rushes down the stairs with the extinguisher. He soaks his sleeves and dunks his cap in the water vessel . . . and stares at the flames.*

PETRUS Christ Almighty!

PETRUS *sprays water avidly onto the flames.* VOGLER, PAULINE, *and* ÅKERBLOM *stand in the doorway, watching.* ÅKERBLOM *has lit his cigarette lighter.*

PAULINE I hope they're insured.

VOGLER The Fire of Doomsday—that's what it is!

PETRUS *tries to douse the last of the flames with his cap.*

HANNA APELBLAD He's done it!

MÄRTA LUNDBERG Yes, as long as he doesn't get burned!

A VOICE The ceiling's on fire, too!

ALGOT FRÖVIK As long as it doesn't collapse!

KARIN BERGMAN Could it?

The flames are extinguished. ALL *applaud.* PETRUS*'s cap has caught fire, but he deals with that swiftly. He is quite winded, coughs, and collapses, thumping his chest. He is helped up by members of the audience.*

HANNA APELBLAD What about a drop of coffee? We could do with that.

CHIEF SUPERINTENDENT I think we've got lots of packets of Christmas tree candles left over.

MRS. BERGLUND There's large packets and small ones and thick ones and stumps and half-burnt ones.

CHIEF SUPERINTENDENT They're left over from the Christmas party.

PAULINE and MÄRTA LUNDBERG start lighting candles. FREDRIK BLOM and VOGLER help. There's a tinkling of chinaware and spoons. ÅKERBLOM, lighter in hand, moves closer to PAULINE.

ÅKERBLOM Listen, play something soothing for them.

PAULINE That's a good idea.

The candles are lighted. Refreshments served. The congregation sits in a circle drinking their coffee. The ambience is subdued. PAULINE plays a piece, to the end. Applause. VOGLER rises and interrupts the clapping:

VOGLER One moment. One moment, my dear audience. May I say a few words? I have a suggestion. Would you honor me by lending my suggestion a willing ear?

ALL very much want to hear his suggestion. A mild cheerfulness begins to spread, as if they had just been spared some threatening, possibly mortal danger. By all means—a suggestion would be nice.

VOGLER Well then. We have a small assembly which has braved the rage of the elements and the evil attack of electrical demons! We have candles, beautiful lighting, I must say. We have creature comforts. There is warmth in the stove. We have music. Let us sit here, on the stage, and let the drama take shape within our midst. What do you say to that? What d'you say?

ÅKERBLOM An excellent suggestion!

After a brief moment, there are murmurs of approval, ALL would seem to be in agreement.

ÅKERBLOM soots a cork in a candle flame, and then, in front of a mirror, gives himself sideburns. PAULINE changes places with him in order to adjust her appearance, and then sits down at the piano and waits.

The myriad candles flicker uneasily, but as the warmth rises they settle down, eventually illuminating the arena in their gentle glow. ÅKERBLOM steps forward, still in his full-length black coat; it has at least the hint of a costume, even if it bears little resemblance to anything.

ÅKERBLOM Let's raise the moon, if you would be so good! Mr. Landahl, moonlight on the bench!

VOGLER raises a yellow moon made of paper, and adjusts it. PETRUS switches on a filtered, battery-powered hand lamp, climbs up a stepladder, and shines it onto the makeshift arena.

ÅKERBLOM Miss Thibault, music!

ÅKERBLOM gives the sign to start playing.

ÅKERBLOM My dear friends, let us imagine the Vienna of 1823, a warm, almost close August evening. We find ourselves in a magnificent palace or rather in the leafy grounds of the palace, where statues shimmer in the twilight and the fountains play. The French windows are open to the twilight, the festive rooms radiant in lights, dance, music, laughter, and hubbub. On a marble seat, Franz Schubert is sitting—I am Franz Schubert—and I am deep in thought. An exquisitely beautiful woman hesitantly, almost timidly, approaches.

PAULINE almost rises, but hesitates, looking to see if she or someone else is to play the part. ÅKERBLOM surfaces from his "thoughts" and looks at PAULINE.

ÅKERBLOM You can come now, Pauline.

PAULINE approaches ÅKERBLOM.

PAULINE—*MIZZI* May I sit down?

SCHUBERT rises reverently.

ÅKERBLOM—*SCHUBERT* Your Grace!

PAULINE—*MIZZI* I've disturbed you.

ÅKERBLOM—*SCHUBERT* Oh, not at all. Please sit here in the moonlight.

PAULINE—*MIZZI* I want to thank you for your music making. You must have been hurt by the indifference of your audience.

ÅKERBLOM—*SCHUBERT* No, no. I am neither sad nor offended. The Count is, moreover, extremely generous. He has even offered to buy my last string quartet for an astonishing sum. Provided he can publish it under his own name, that is.

PAULINE—*MIZZI* But Herr Schubert, how can you allow . . .

ÅKERBLOM—*SCHUBERT* I can write another one. Count von Schweinitz cannot.

PAULINE—*MIZZI* A secret, Herr Schubert. I'm not a countess at all.

ÅKERBLOM—*SCHUBERT* Is Madame Countess not a countess?

PAULINE—*MIZZI* I'm just a little whore.

ÅKERBLOM—*SCHUBERT* But that's . . . that's not . . .

PAULINE—*MIZZI* My stepfather has just sold me to Baron Siraudon.

ÅKERBLOM—*SCHUBERT* Baron Siraudon?

PAULINE—*MIZZI* The one with all those comedies and those funny farces. He's colossally rich and owns two palaces in Hungary, four vineyards in Provence, and apartments in London and Vienna. I'm to live in one of those apartments.

ÅKERBLOM—*SCHUBERT* I see.

PAULINE—*MIZZI* (*sensibly*) The Baron's buying me did me good. I can't say he's particularly kind, but he has taught me things.

ÅKERBLOM—*SCHUBERT* So Baron Siraudon bought you?

PAULINE—*MIZZI* A doctor examined me and certified that I was a virgin. My stepfather gave me two and a half percent of the sum of purchase, which was nice of him, I must say.

ÅKERBLOM—*SCHUBERT* Well, yes . . . indeed, indeed.

PAULINE—*MIZZI* But by far the nicest part of it all—I am still a virgin.

ÅKERBLOM—*SCHUBERT* How considerate of Baron Siraudon.

ÅKERBLOM suddenly stiffens, then turns and stares straight ahead. The red drapes part slightly, revealing the CLOWN, who looks at him through the gap. ÅKERBLOM closes his eyes. The CLOWN vanishes and ÅKERBLOM sighs heavily.

PAULINE—*MIZZI* Now the moon has gone behind a cloud and it's getting windy.

ÅKERBLOM—*SCHUBERT* Perhaps we should go in?

PAULINE—*MIZZI* No, Herr Schubert. Let's stay out here. I like it when the wind rustles the oak trees down by the banks of the river.

SCHUBERT chuckles.

ÅKERBLOM—*SCHUBERT* Yes. That's it.

PAULINE—*MIZZI* You laugh?

ÅKERBLOM—*SCHUBERT* I was thinking: We're both bought and sold, Miss Mizzi.

PAULINE—*MIZZI* I'm sure to have been much more expensive. Not counting rent, servants, wardrobe, and carriage. I actually feel quite proud when I think how costly I am. At least five thousand guilders!

ÅKERBLOM—*SCHUBERT* I won't disclose the price of my quartet. May I hold your hand?

PAULINE—*MIZZI* You bite your nails, Herr Schubert.

MIZZI quickly kisses his hand. Out of the woods, VOGLER emerges, wearing a top hat; a sweeping black topcoat is unbuttoned over a white dress shirt. In his hand, a light walking stick.

VOGLER—*SIRAUDON* So there you are, my wild dove!

PAULINE—*MIZZI* Forgive me, Baron Siraudon. But it was so hot in the ballroom and I think I have a slight fever. This is . . .

VOGLER—*SIRAUDON* Wouldn't I be able to recognize our beloved maestro? All Vienna is singing his songs. A pleasure to make your acquaintance.

ÅKERBLOM—*SCHUBERT* A singularly great pleasure, Baron Siraudon.

VOGLER—*SIRAUDON* An appropriate meeting! This afternoon I attended a rehearsal of my latest comedy, *Women's Whims*, delightfully played, particularly by Madame Sassari. When I complimented her, she complained.

ÅKERBLOM—*SCHUBERT* And what was troubling the great actress?

VOGLER—*SIRAUDON* She sings a little song, only a few lines. They recur in every act. It's her signature tune, if you take my point, Herr Schubert.

SCHUBERT bows.

ÅKERBLOM—*SCHUBERT* Indeed I do, Herr Baron.

VOGLER—*SIRAUDON* It goes like this: "My little puss, what would'st of me? My little puss, my little puss, I do love thee."

ÅKERBLOM—*SCHUBERT* Enchanting poetry.

VOGLER—*SIRAUDON* The composer is but an able craftsman. He has not grasped the subtle obscenity of the poem. I ask you quite straightforwardly: Can you help me?

SCHUBERT sings quietly though somewhat hoarsely.

ÅKERBLOM—*SCHUBERT* "My little puss what would'st of me? My little puss, my little puss, I do love thee."

SCHUBERT has sung his suggested version.

ÅKERBLOM—*SCHUBERT* Something like that?

VOGLER—*SIRAUDON* It's true what they say . . . you are a master. Would you have the goodness to write down the music?

ÅKERBLOM—*SCHUBERT* It'll be done in a moment, Herr Baron.

VOGLER—*SIRAUDON* Your fee?

ÅKERBLOM—*SCHUBERT* At your pleasure, Herr Baron.

SCHUBERT leaves. SIRAUDON turns to MIZZI, threateningly:

VOGLER—*SIRAUDON* I'll teach you to run off!

PAULINE—*MIZZI* Not here, Paul. Not here. Not now.

VOGLER—*SIRAUDON* I find you in the arms of that filthy cross-eyed musician.

PAULINE—*MIZZI* Forgive me. Forgive me.

VOGLER—*SIRAUDON* You're to rinse your mouth out with tincture of iodine. Then we shall cleanse ourselves with a rose enema. But first we'll go for a little ride.

PAULINE—*MIZZI* But not here!

VOGLER—*SIRAUDON* Yes, here! À cheval, mademoiselle!

SIRAUDON pushes MIZZI down on all fours, then repeatedly strikes her on the the back with his stick. She whimpers. SCHUBERT has witnessed the scene and stands there, his arms hanging.

ÅKERBLOM—*SCHUBERT* Excuse me. I'm still here, as it happens.

VOGLER—*SIRAUDON* Oh, you're here, are you? I didn't see.

SIRAUDON gets out his wallet.

VOGLER—*SIRAUDON* A small acknowledgement for your little tune.

SIRAUDON fishes a coin out of the wallet and throws it to the ground at his feet.

VOGLER—*SIRAUDON* Here you are.

ÅKERBLOM—*SCHUBERT* Thank you, Herr Baron.

SCHUBERT picks up the coin.

VOGLER—*SIRAUDON* Get up, Miss Veith. Arrange your attire. We are to dance the evening's pavane with candelabras, and we're not to give in. Give me your hand, Miss Veith. Farewell, Maestro. I remember your delightful tune perfectly.

ÅKERBLOM Franz Schubert stood in the dark outside the tall windows and watched the stately dance, weeping with humilation and sudden insight. That ends Act One. Those wishing to applaud may do so now.

ÅKERBLOM beckons VOGLER and PAULINE in; they take a curtain call as the AUDIENCE applauds.

ÅKERBLOM And now we change scene. Would the audience be so kind as to sit here.

ÅKERBLOM points.

ÅKERBLOM The piano there.

The members of the AUDIENCE pick up their chairs and move. MRS. APELBLAD takes a few steps on her chubby legs and breaks the silence.

HANNA APELBLAD Anyone want another cup? There's plenty of coffee in the thermoses.

The SPECTATORS find their feet and start moving in various directions. PETRUS pushes the pianino into position. More pastries are taken, more coffee is poured, and more coal is hoppered into the stove. MÄRTA LUNDBERG has dug a book, tattered from reading, out of her bag, and moves closer to KARIN BERGMAN to read something, which we cannot hear for the increasingly benevolent hubbub. The CHIEF SUPERINTENDENT goes up to PAULINE, who is behind a screen, changing costume.

CHIEF SUPERINTENDENT Are there many acts? I'm meant to be home by eleven.

PAULINE Oh, no. We've done one act and the next two acts are not that long.

CHIEF SUPERINTENDENT I wasn't asking because it was dull.

MRS. APELBLAD has a Danish pastry in her hand and glares at the CHIEF SUPERINTENDENT.

CHIEF SUPERINTENDENT No, thank you. No pastry for me.

FREDRIK BLOM sits in VOGLER's place, next to ÅKERBLOM.

FREDRIK BLOM In the end, Schubert must have realized how he was to form the last movement of his great symphony.

ÅKERBLOM Oh, yes, of course. Excuse us.

FREDRIK BLOM Yes, of course.

PETRUS strikes the gong. The SPECTATORS have taken their seats. When eveyone else has quieted down, MÄRTA LUNDBERG is agitated, but determined, her voice trembling at first, then steadying to a sturdy sound.

MÄRTA LUNDBERG Before the play continues, if I may, I would like to read something I found long ago in a book. To put it short, it is the story of a young man seeking his way. It's as if the actual seeking had become the main point and was concealing what he was seeking. And now I shall read what the author has written:

MÄRTA LUNDBERG rises.

MÄRTA LUNDBERG "You complain that you cry out and that God does not reply. You say that you are locked in, and you are afraid it is a life sentence, although no one has said anything. Consider then, that you are your own judge and your own jailer. Prisoner, walk from your prison! To your astonishment, you will find that no one will stop you. The reality outside prison is indeed terrifying, but never as terrifying as your anguish, way down there in that locked room. Take your first step toward freedom. It is not difficult. But, though the second step is more difficult, never allow yourself to be defeated by your jailer, who is only your own fear and your own pride." Well, that's all, then.

MÄRTA LUNDBERG has read most of it from the opened book, but toward the end she has raised her eyes, which have been watery. She sits down, slightly embarrassed.

HANNA APELBLAD Wouldn't you like a drop of coffee, Märta?

MÄRTA LUNDBERG Thank you kindly, Hanna.

MÄRTA LUNDBERG whispers to MRS. APELBLAD.

MÄRTA LUNDBERG Sweet Jesus, I should never've read that.

ÅKERBLOM Now we must begin Act Two. This is what it looks like: Behind a screen covered with ragged cloth we find Schubert's simple resting place. Beneath the right-hand skylight, we can see an iron stove on which there are unwashed utensils of the simplest kind, and a pianino, a few chairs, and a broken table. Now, good people, I hope you can imagine all that, as well as the unendurable stench of mold, dirt, and the primitive medicaments the maestro is forced to take to alleviate his smoldering decay. A good friend is visiting, Marcus Jacobi, the organist, respected by all.

The two MUSICIANS play four-handed the last bars of the last movement of the ninth symphony.

ÅKERBLOM—*SCHUBERT* Well? You won't say anything?

VOGLER—*JACOBI* You must give me a little breathing space.

ÅKERBLOM—*SCHUBERT* You're my friend, Jacobi. We've played right through the symphony together. You are the only person I have confided in.

VOGLER—*JACOBI* It's a work of size.

ÅKERBLOM—*SCHUBERT* Yes, great, is it not? My greatest.

VOGLER—*JACOBI* I mean long.

ÅKERBLOM—*SCHUBERT* Long?

VOGLER—*JACOBI* As your friend, I must be honest.

ÅKERBLOM—*SCHUBERT* You don't like my symphony.

VOGLER—*JACOBI* The beginning is brilliant.

ÅKERBLOM—*SCHUBERT* That doesn't console me.

JACOBI is gentle in his criticism.

VOGLER—*JACOBI* I am not here to say consoling words.

ÅKERBLOM—*SCHUBERT* Forgive me.

VOGLER—*JACOBI* You told me you were looking for a good teacher, so you could acquire a little education in composing. What has become of that?

ÅKERBLOM—*SCHUBERT* I lacked the courage . . . and the money.

VOGLER—*JACOBI* Such a pity, Schubert. Your symphony suffers from the most terrible faults. As I see it, the violins and wood-wind are unplayable. And what is this? It sounds like some sort of baroque!

ÅKERBLOM—*SCHUBERT* It's meant to sound baroque.

VOGLER—*JACOBI* Yes, yes. And the last movement! It seems demented.

ÅKERBLOM—*SCHUBERT* That is the intention.

VOGLER—*JACOBI* How many times—in this nagging, champing eternity—do you repeat the main theme?

ÅKERBLOM—*SCHUBERT* I haven't counted.

VOGLER—*JACOBI* You must forgive me my candidness. I may be wrong. You must allow for my being wrong.

ÅKERBLOM—*SCHUBERT* The theme, the main theme, the constantly recurring theme is a cry . . . of joy! I stood here at my desk and I couldn't avoid . . .

SCHUBERT makes an effort to sound matter-of-fact.

ÅKERBLOM—*SCHUBERT* . . . I couldn't avoid, at each instant, feeling in my body, in my flesh, in my nerves, in my sex, in my muscles, in my brain, in the terrifying racing of my heart, how my disease was grinding and burrowing away, how those repulsive medicaments were poisoning my nerves, every single minute. I was in hell. But God sent me this cry of joy, this cry that is so short. And it alleviated . . . made the pain insignificant, made my illness meaningless, and made the raging of the medicines into distant echoes. I thought that . . . My intention was to . . . I thought that other people, tormented by their hellish humiliation as I am tormented . . . I thought I would cry out to them as to myself. And I cry out so often and so long that the pain becomes unreal and the disease a phantom.

VOGLER—*JACOBI* Music of major proportions has never been your music, Schubert. You are no Beethoven; you are Franz Schubert, and that's fine as it is.

ÅKERBLOM—*SCHUBERT* But what revisions ought I to undertake?

VOGLER—*JACOBI* I can give you one piece of advice only.

ÅKERBLOM—*SCHUBERT* I understand.

VOGLER—*JACOBI* Forgive me.

ÅKERBLOM—*SCHUBERT* Don't ask me to forgive you, Frère Jacobi! You have done your friend the greatest of favors.

VOGLER—*JACOBI* I must leave.

ÅKERBLOM—*SCHUBERT* You have spoken the truth.

VOGLER—*JACOBI* I must leave—I have a service at three o'clock.

ÅKERBLOM—*SCHUBERT* Farewell, my friend.

VOGLER—*JACOBI* Farewell.

SCHUBERT and JACOBI shake hands and embrace. JACOBI retreats into the twilight outside the acting arena. SCHUBERT sits down again, turning over pages of the score.

ÅKERBLOM—*SCHUBERT* I am sinking, sinking.

PETRUS gives PAULINE a bouquet of artificial flowers and "knocks" on the set.

ÅKERBLOM—*SCHUBERT* Enter, if you please!

MIZZI has brought SCHUBERT a bouquet. MIZZI feigns happiness.

PAULINE—*MIZZI* Good evening, dear Franz. Here you are, moping away in the dusk although it's such heavenly spring weather. Can we not go for a little walk? Not far, no farther than you feel you can manage.

ÅKERBLOM—*SCHUBERT* You're happy, Mizzi?

MIZZI gives him the flowers.

PAULINE—*MIZZI* Happy name's day!

ÅKERBLOM—*SCHUBERT* You must sit yourself down and tell me . . . I can see that something has happened.

PAULINE—*MIZZI* I have given the great Paul Siraudon the boot. Good-bye, Baron Siraudon with all your comedies and farces and rose enemas and whips.

ÅKERBLOM—*SCHUBERT* What does your stepfather say?

PAULINE—*MIZZI* At this moment my lord stepfather is trekking his way through a letter telling him of the state of matters and my very own decisions!

ÅKERBLOM—*SCHUBERT* A letter. You can hardly write your own name.

MIZZI smiles inwardly.

PAULINE—*MIZZI* I dictated it.

ÅKERBLOM—*SCHUBERT* And who took down your dictation?

PAULINE—*MIZZI* A student.

ÅKERBLOM—*SCHUBERT* A student?

PAULINE—*MIZZI* Don't keep asking silly questions, Franz.

ÅKERBLOM—*SCHUBERT* Love?

PAULINE—*MIZZI* The one, great, all-embracing love.

ÅKERBLOM—*SCHUBERT* Can he support you?

PAULINE—*MIZZI* He can hardly support himself. But I have temporary employment in the chorus—at the Volkstheater.

ÅKERBLOM—*SCHUBERT* You have your jewels.

PAULINE—*MIZZI* I've given them back, one and all!

ÅKERBLOM—*SCHUBERT* And what did Herr Baron say?

PAULINE—*MIZZI* I was at once to be given the key if I did all the things he likes best. And so I did, as I was in a hurry. But then he wouldn't let me out, although he'd promised, and he gave me a beating. Would you like to see my backside, Franz. It's actually extremely colorful.

ÅKERBLOM—*SCHUBERT* No. No, thank you, Mizzi dear. No thank you.

PAULINE—*MIZZI* As soon as I was out, in that great windy park with its avenues down to the Danube, I was so insanely cheerful I shrieked out loud: "I can do as I please!" And the first thing I wanted to do was pick those flowers and race over here to wish you a happy name's day and tell you about everything that had happened to me in the space of just a few hours.

ÅKERBLOM—*SCHUBERT* And the student?

PAULINE—*MIZZI* He has lectures all day, so we can't meet until this evening.

SCHUBERT looks in his wallet and finds a note.

ÅKERBLOM—*SCHUBERT* Might I perhaps contribute to the evening's delights.

PAULINE—*MIZZI* You're the very sweetest, very dearest . . .

MIZZI hugs SCHUBERT.

PAULINE—*MIZZI* I must be allowed to kiss you, my dearest Franz.

ÅKERBLOM looks rapidly sideways, rises slowly with fear in his eyes. In the doorway the CLOWN appears, her mouth twitching slightly, only to disappear again . . .

ÅKERBLOM No, no, no . . . No, no.

ÅKERBLOM begins suddenly to weep. It is not Schubert crying; it is Carl Åkerblom. He falls into a chair and then to the floor, sobbing, taking off his glasses and rubbing his eyes with his knuckles. KARIN BERGMAN crouches down over an ÅKERBLOM in tears.

KARIN Pull yourself together, Carl. Carl, I know you can. If you want to. And I know you want to. Carl, listen now. There's nothing to be afraid of, nothing to be afraid of.

KARIN rests her head on ÅKERBLOM's, as if invoking a power to make him rise, and ÅKERBLOM does rise, obediently if somewhat clumsily.

ÅKERBLOM I do so apologize . . . I do apologize. I don't know what came over me. I am usually of an extremely controlled nature.

ÅKERBLOM wipes his nose.

ÅKERBLOM I thought we might go on now and bring our drama to a close—here.

ÅKERBLOM points at a spot on the floor.

PAULINE starts playing. ÅKERBLOM sits in a rocking chair on "runners." He has wrapped a rug around his legs and put a small cushion behind his head.

VOGLER It is now autumn and the leaves on the trees in the parks of Vienna have all fallen. Franz Schubert is seriously ill and is living on alms from his brother Ferdinand. That is the situation on this cloudy gray Thursday afternoon at the end of October. I am sure that we all remember the beginning of our cinema performance. Now we are there again: same pictures, same misery, same words! That is, Schubert saying: "You came after all, my darling Mizzi!"

ÅKERBLOM moves his lips whispering the same line. PETRUS is high up on the ladder and beats the gong. ÅKERBLOM as SCHUBERT closes his eyes and breathes slowly, coughing occasionally. PAULINE as MIZZI comes in without knocking.

PAULINE—*MIZZI* Come whatever may, you must know that I love you, my dear Franz.

ÅKERBLOM—*SCHUBERT* Mizzi, my little Mizzi . . . Mizzi, here is my last sonata. Would you be kind enough to hand the material over to my brother Ferdinand. And now, you are to go. I've fouled myself and vomited and the smell is abominable.

PAULINE—*MIZZI* I am here to say farewell. My student and I are traveling to Paris. We leave in a few hours.

ÅKERBLOM—*SCHUBERT* Such joy!

PAULINE—*MIZZI* Farewell, my dear beloved, poor Franz.

MIZZI hugs him fiercely, disappears from the arena, and goes straight to the piano, where she sits down and plays "Impromptu 142, No 1" in f-minor, perhaps not all of it, but a minute or so of it. The music stops when "Count" Marcell VEITH steps forward. He (OSVALD VOGLER) is dignified and terrifying.

VOGLER—*VEITH* Herr Schubert?

ÅKERBLOM—*SCHUBERT* To whom do I owe this honor?

VOGLER—*VEITH* Count Marcell Veith, with your permission. Little Mizzi's stepfather.

VEITH sits down beside the sick man, takes a dazzlingly white handkerchief out of his coat pocket and a small perfume flask from the folds of his tailcoat, splashes a few drops onto his handkerchief, and holds it to his long nose.

VOGLER—*VEITH* Ghastly! There is no God. My step-daughter . . .

ÅKERBLOM—*SCHUBERT* I am dying. Please show my humiliating condition respect, Herr Count Veith, by speaking the truth.

VOGLER—*VEITH* Mizzi, my poor child, my little girl, has taken her life.

ÅKERBLOM—*SCHUBERT* She . . . She was so happy.

VOGLER—*VEITH* And the blame for her death rests on you, Herr Schubert.

ÅKERBLOM—*SCHUBERT* Blame? Blame? What blame?

VOGLER—*VEITH* She loved you with the fierce passion of a young woman and was prepared to throw everything away: a brilliant career, a wonderful lover. She rejected a father's love. Everything, Herr Schubert, she threw away in her blind love for a wretched musician. Yesterday at half past ten in the morning, my servant announced visitors. I went out into the vestibule and there met two police officers in civilian clothing, and as considerately as possible they informed me of the terrible news: my daughter had been found under Tegenbrücke, where she had caught on a wooden bridge pier.

ÅKERBLOM—*SCHUBERT* But the student?

VOGLER—*VEITH* I don't understand what you're talking about. What student?

ÅKERBLOM—*SCHUBERT* How can you know . . .

VOGLER—*VEITH* Very simple, Herr Schubert, and terrifyingly evident.

VEITH takes out a little book with gilt clasp and garlands on the soft binding.

VOGLER—*VEITH* My daughter kept a combined diary and account book. Here it is; please read it.

SCHUBERT takes the book, leafs through it, reads.

VOGLER—*VEITH* Read and consider. And let shame's red flush flare in those cheeks of yours, so ravaged by debauchery.

SCHUBERT tears off his spectacles, which fall to the ground, and he hides his face in his hand.

VOGLER— *VEITH* If I didn't know that you were soon to die from the terrible torments that punish the rake, I would challenge you to a duel. But I have no desire to reduce your suffering. A harsh God holds his hand over your head, Mr. Musician. "Revenge is mine, saith the Lord."

VOGLER interrupts himself as Veith, without a pause.

VOGLER Excuse me . . . Please excuse me. Some courteous gentlemen are waiting for me outside that door. They have been sent out into the winter night by my wife in consultation with Dr. Egerman. Their task is to gather up what is left of Osvald Vogler and then deliver him into the security of the asylum. How many times have not people, in their madness, locked the prophets away in their prisons?

ÅKERBLOM Osvald.

VOGLER But we have as yet never called on the hosts of angels. The rustle of their wings has not yet reached the ears of those foolish children—mankind—with the exception of a few. I am thinking, in the first place, of Beethoven . . . So there is testimony!

PAULINE Stop now, Osvald!

VOGLER No! Let me finish!

Two POLICEMEN walk in.

VOGLER One day darkness will thunder over the cities. One day. One day the worms will eat into your rotting bodies. Your entrails will come out of your shameful orifices, out of those that exist and out of those that the angels of the great dragon have torn open from your entrails. Umm . . . I'm cold. May I have my overcoat?

MÄRTA LUNDBERG Mr. Vogler?

VOGLER No, there's no defense!

MÄRTA LUNDBERG Mr. Vogler, you're talking about the wrong day.

VOGLER is astonished.

VOGLER Am I talking about the wrong day?

MÄRTA LUNDBERG Yes . . . quite wrong.

MÄRTA LUNDBERG moves up to him.

VOGLER But all my wrath? What shall I do with all my justifiable wrath?

MÄRTA LUNDBERG Poor, poor Mr. Vogler.

MÄRTA LUNDBERG pats him on the cheek.

MÄRTA LUNDBERG Here, Mr. Vogler, are your hat and overcoat.

MÄRTA LUNDBERG puts the hat on VOGLER's head.

PAULINE Farewell then, Osvald.

PAULINE kisses VOGLER.

PAULINE Where are his galoshes?

ÅKERBLOM We forgot them in Avesta.

VOGLER is escorted from the Good Templar Hall. More coal is poured into the stove. The moon shines brightly.

ALGOT FRÖVIK The storm has died down.

KARIN BERGMAN Well, how is it to be? Is the play over?

ÅKERBLOM What? Yes, yes of course. You mean the cinema performance? The cinema performance is virtually at its end.

MRS. BERGLUND wakes up.

MRS. BERGLUND Is it already over?

KARIN PERSSON But is there anything left?

ÅKERBLOM A little, but not much. Pauline is to play a few bars—play the end, please—and then there's a tight close-up of the dying maestro, who is looking straight at the audience, roughly like this.

ÅKERBLOM "frames" his head between two arms.

ÅKERBLOM And then we have to imagine the wretched, evil-smelling room filling with a mysterious light. When he hears the wonderful music, he smiles although he is so tired, and he says . . . then he says:

ÅKERBLOM masters his emotions . . .

ÅKERBLOM—*(SCHUBERT)* "I'm sinking." Then he is silent for a few moments, listening to . . . his own impromptu. Then he says as clear as clear: "I'm not sinking, I'm not sinking . . . I'm rising." Then the picture darkens and the music ends . . . and, well, that's the end of our cinema film.

ALL applaud.

CHIEF SUPERINTENDENT Time to be going home, then.

HANNA APELBLAD And to say thanks very much and good-bye.

The members of the AUDIENCE put on their outdoor clothes. MRS. BERGLUND shakes hands and excuses herself.

MRS. BERGLUND Well, goodnight and thanks ever so. I must have nodded off, as I'm up milking at half past five, so I get a bit tired of an evening. But it was so . . . Thank you and goodnight. Oh, yes: I can come and lend a hand in the morning; just telephone. Grånäs twelve is the number.

MÄRTA LUNDBERG has been standing to one side, but suddenly makes a decision, turns to PAULINE.

MÄRTA LUNDBERG Goodnight, I'll be in to help with the packing in the morning before half past seven, but then I've got school.

MÄRTA LUNDBERG holds out her book.

MÄRTA LUNDBERG I want to give you this book, Miss Thibault. It's not in such good condition—there's underlining and it's dog-eared.

PAULINE Thank you.

CHIEF SUPERINTENDENT It'll be a cold night, so keep the stove going.

HANNA APELBLAD It'll certainly reach thirty below. You can see, from the moonlight.

The CHIEF SUPERINTENDENT waits by the door.

CHIEF SUPERINTENDENT Come on, Hanna. We can walk together.

HANNA APELBLAD Good-bye, then.

PETRUS We can pack the projector tomorrow morning. I'll be here in good time with the lorry. The goods train to Insjön doesn't usually get to Grånäs until quarter past nine.

PETRUS shakes hands.

PETRUS Well, Mr. Åkerblom . . . Shall I wake the organist? He's fallen asleep on the bench there.

FREDRIK BLOM No, I'm not asleep. Thank you for the lovely music, Miss. Personally, I interpret Schubert's impromptus differently. That's not meant as criticism. It was lovely, anyway, though somewhat feminine for my taste, but absolutely beautiful. Thank you!

KARIN PERSSON Good-bye and thank you. Good-bye and thank you.

PAULINE Thank you.

KARIN PERSSON Wait a moment, Bloomy, so we can leave together. We're going the same way.

BLOM the organist waits by the door.

KARIN PERSSON Put your earmuffs on.

KARIN PERSSON and FREDRIK BLOM vanish through the narrow door, which lets in heavy breaths of bitingly cold air.

ALGOT FRÖVIK This has been a tremendous experience of true art. Forgive me for saying so, but the theater was much better than the cinema. Thank you once again. Good-bye.

PAULINE is counting the takings. KARIN BERGMAN is waiting to one side. She is the last of the audience.

ÅKERBLOM Goodnight, Little Sis, and thank you for coming.

KARIN BERGMAN And thank you. Thank you for a splendid evening. I have a mesage from Mumsey for you both.

ÅKERBLOM Have you? It's bound to be nasty.

PAULINE Don't be so difficult, Mr. Åkerblom. I have just counted our takings this evening and it comes to eight kronor and eighty öre.

ÅKERBLOM Well, that wasn't too bad!

PAULINE sighs.

ÅKERBLOM And the message?

KARIN BERGMAN Yes: "If it were to suit Miss Thibault and Carl to spend the night at home with us, they would be heartily welcome to do so."

PAULINE How very kind of Mrs. Åkerblom.

ÅKERBLOM I'd never grant that devilish woman such a triumph—you can tell her from me.

KARIN BERGMAN laughs.

KARIN BERGMAN That I cannot tell her!

ÅKERBLOM And in the morning the loony would be transported to the asylum, under the guidance of Gustaf-Adolf. Thanks a lot.

KARIN BERGMAN Gustaf-Adolf is in Florence with his new wife, as you well know. Mama and I and old Miss Nilsson and the boys make up the entire complement at the summer residence.

ÅKERBLOM So you've got the boys with you?

KARIN BERGMAN Mmm. Come and do some conjuring, Charlie. You know what fun it'd be. Like last winter.

ÅKERBLOM Then I could . . . Well, what do you say, Pauline?

PAULINE I'll say nothing—to avoid any argument.

ÅKERBLOM sighs, thinking.

ÅKERBLOM Please thank our mother for her impeccably friendly invitation, but tell her it came too late.

KARIN BERGMAN kisses ÅKERBLOM on the cheek.

KARIN BERGMAN Good-bye, Carl. Sleep well.

ÅKERBLOM strokes her cheek with his hand, and then moves his hand to cover his mouth. PAULINE moves toward the door and KARIN follows her. They do not stop on the way, do not pause, do not say a word about the moonlight or Karin's boys. Just polite smiles, then the door is closed and the key is turned in the lock.

Scene 3

ÅKERBLOM is asleep on the cot, snoring quietly and irregularly. PAULINE has made herself comfortable in the armchair. Not many candles are still alight. The moonlight is whitish, painting a harsh pattern on the cluttered floor. From the stove there's a faint rumbling. Otherwise the silence is like a pillar of dark metal reaching all the way up to eternity.

The CLOWN appears from behind a cupboard and moves sideways along the windows.

ÅKERBLOM No, no.

ÅKERBLOM sits up.

ÅKERBLOM No, no. Pauline, are you awake?

No reply.

ÅKERBLOM Why don't you answer? Are you angry about something?

Silence. PAULINE remains motionless.

ÅKERBLOM Are you really going to send me back to the asylum . . . when all this is really over?

PAULINE Come here, come here.

ÅKERBLOM sits on a chair and leans his head against her breast.

ÅKERBLOM You're going to leave me.

PAULINE I am not going to leave you.

ÅKERBLOM You're lying.

ÅKERBLOM trudges about, biting his thumbnail. The white rays of moonlight lacerate the room. The stove sighs now and again; otherwise all is still.

PAULINE You never know when I'm lying. So it would be more practical to believe what I say. And I'm saying I have no intention of ever leaving you.

ÅKERBLOM You're lying again.

PAULINE All right, then I am.

ÅKERBLOM You'll make certain I'm locked up.

PAULINE Please, can't we stop now?

ÅKERBLOM imitating her.

ÅKERBLOM "Please, can't we stop now?"

PAULINE Do as you like.

ÅKERBLOM still imitating.

ÅKERBLOM "Do as you like."

PAULINE Just don't think I'm afraid.

ÅKERBLOM imitating again.

ÅKERBLOM "Just don't think I'm afraid."

PAULINE For Christ's sake! *For Christ's sake!*

ÅKERBLOM takes a few swift silent steps toward the bed and grasps PAULINE by the arms. She resists feebly. He drags her to the floor, they trip and fall. He is quickest, and grabs her head in both hands; she whimpers faintly and tries to free herself, but lets her arms fall. ÅKERBLOM very powerfully, yet quietly, says:

ÅKERBLOM Look at me! Look at me!

Then ÅKERBLOM yells:

ÅKERBLOM *Look at me!*

PAULINE and ÅKERBLOM are motionless. This madman is moreover a strong man; Carl could certainly break this girl's skull, crush her temples or push her eyes in. PAULINE, unmoving, now heavy, does not look at him; she keeps her eyes closed. The moon shines. Twice, the pressure is increased on her head; he breathes, panting, audibly, between silences.

PAULINE Am I to die now?

ÅKERBLOM Perhaps we are both to die.

PAULINE That'll be all right.

ÅKERBLOM's hands relinquish their grip, and they kneel opposite each other, their faces very close, for a long while.

PAULINE gets up. ÅKERBLOM reaches out a finger to touch her. She slaps it back, as if trying to swat a fly. ÅKERBLOM sits down on the bed, PAULINE in the armchair.

PAULINE Just don't reproach me. Nor yourself, for that matter.

ÅKERBLOM No. I would like to say that my stepmother is an extremely charming lady.

PAULINE That's what you usually say.

ÅKERBLOM My little sister Karin would probably have woken her boys and they would have come sleepily out of the nursery and at once asked whether I was going to do some conjuring . . . or something else we usually make up to do together, and I would have said that this evening it is much too late, but tomorrow . . . tomorrow we'll look at the moving pictures. Then we would have sat down under the brass lamp in the dining room and the boys would have been there and we would have drunk stepmother's elderberry wine and helped ourselves to marinated herring and scrambled sprat and liver pâté with gherkins and cold meatballs and boiled ham and poached eggs and, best of all, Miss Nilsson's game pâté. Then when we'd had enough we would to help clear the dishes and then we would sit for a while by the fire until only the embers were left, by which time the boys would have fallen asleep and I would carry them into the nursery, *my* nursery—for Christ's sake, it's *my* nursery, Pauline! Then we would have sat for a little while longer by the fire . . . no. No, no. No. First stepmother would have taken you by the wrist and said she was grateful that you had taken responsibilty for me.

ÅKERBLOM catches a glimpse of a figure in the darkness: the CLOWN. *They look each other in the eye. The* CLOWN *moves behind a flat.*

Everything is quite still.

The moonlight produces a high purring tone, hardly audible, which comes and goes, returning louder now, then weaker . . . The boards, dirty, reflect the cold light onto the walls and ceiling and onto the scenery birch trees.

CARL ÅKERBLOM *takes a pair of scissors from under the pillow, and pushes the points against the artery in his wrist.*

PAULINE If you die, I don't want to live any longer. I want you to know that. Are you listening?

ÅKERBLOM lifts his head a bit.

PAULINE You know you can wake me whenever you feel like it.

ÅKERBLOM By the way, she is already here.

PAULINE Who is here?

ÅKERBLOM Listen, and you will hear.

ÅKERBLOM lies back down on the bed.

PAULINE listens.

A pair of scissors are heard falling onto the floor.

PAULINE I can't hear anything.

ÅKERBLOM You sink . . . sink . . . You really do.

PAULINE walks over to the bed and lies down on ÅKERBLOM. She moves a hand up to his eyes, and then her hand . . . closes them.

Original translation from the Swedish by Joan Tate, revised, according to the final script of the broadcast version, by Jonathan Mair.

TRANSLATOR'S NOTES

1. The phrase used (*"såsom i en spegel"*) served as the Swedish title of Bergman's film *Through a Mirror Darkly*.
2. August Strindberg.
3. The name "Törneman," literally translated, would be "Thorn Man."
4. "Rigmor" is not an uncommon girl's name in Scandinavia. The pun here is on rigor mortis.
5. A pianino is a shortened piano, often resembling a table (they are sometimes called table pianos) and with fewer octaves to its register than a full piano's.
6. The original Swedish title (*Glädjeflickans glädje*) is a play on "joy" (*glädje*). An alternative translation is: "Joys of a Fille de Joie."
7. The place name Grånäs, literally translated, would be "Gray Ness" or "Gray Point."
8. Stenbjörka, Storforsa, Videvik, and Mörktjärn are all unexotic places in Sweden, as are . . .
9. . . . Besna and Lännheden (see note 8).
10. A riksdaler here means a krona. In the 1920s, 72,000 riksdalers was more than necessary to be the equivalent of a dollar millionaire in the 1990s.